Fresh Ways with
Cakes

COVER
Lightly poached apricots framed with piped whipped cream top a triangular layered sponge cake (recipe, page 74). To keep calories and fat levels down, the sponge is made without butter or margarine: it contains simply eggs, sugar and flour, with lemon rind for flavour.

TIME-LIFE BOOKS

EUROPEAN EDITOR: Ellen Phillips
Design Director: Ed Skyner
Director of Editorial Resources: Louise Tulip
Chief Sub-Editor: Ilse Gray

LOST CIVILIZATIONS
HOW THINGS WORK
SYSTEM EARTH
LIBRARY OF CURIOUS AND
UNUSUAL FACTS
BUILDING BLOCKS
A CHILD'S FIRST LIBRARY OF LEARNING
VOYAGE THROUGH THE UNIVERSE
THE THIRD REICH
MYSTERIES OF THE UNKNOWN
TIME-LIFE HISTORY OF THE WORLD
FITNESS, HEALTH & NUTRITION
HEALTHY HOME COOKING
UNDERSTANDING COMPUTERS
THE ENCHANTED WORLD
LIBRARY OF NATIONS
PLANET EARTH
THE GOOD COOK
THE WORLD'S WILD PLACES

ISBN 0 7054 2002 7
TIME-LIFE is a trademark of Time Warner Inc. U.S.A.

HEALTHY HOME COOKING

SERIES EDITOR: Jackie Matthews
Picture Editor: Mark Karras
Editorial Assistant: Eugénie Romer

Editorial Staff for *Fresh Ways with Cakes:*
Editor: Gillian Moore
Researcher: Susie Dawson
Designer: Mary Staples
Sub-Editor: Wendy Gibbons

EDITORIAL PRODUCTION FOR THE SERIES:
Chief: Maureen Kelly
Assistant: Samantha Hill
Editorial Department: Theresa John, Debra Lelliott

THE CONTRIBUTORS

ROSEMARY WADEY is an authority on home baking. She is a frequent contributor to cookery magazines and the author of many cookbooks, including *Delectable Cakes, Breads and Pastries, Biscuits and Bakes,* and *Cooking for Christmas.*

CAROL BOWEN, who has a degree in home economics, has specialized in creating recipes for the microwave oven. Her publications include *Complete Microwave Cookery* and *Microwave Cooking for One and Two.*

CAROLE HANDSLIP is a cookery writer and broadcaster with a particular interest in healthy eating; the volumes she has written include, *Wholefood Cookery* and *Vegetarian Cookery.* She has taught at the Cordon Bleu Cookery School in London.

JANICE MURFITT trained as a home economist and worked as a cookery editor on *Family Circle* magazine. Her primary interest now is developing recipes for cakes and pastries; her titles include *Cake Icing and Decorating* and *Cheesecakes and Flans.*

JANE SUTHERING is a cookery writer and home economist who has concentrated on desserts, cakes and recipes using wholefoods. Her books include *Step-by-Step Cake Decorating* and she is consultant to Cranks, the health food restaurant chain.

THE COOKS

The recipes in this book were cooked for photography by Pat Alburey, Allyson Birch, Carole Handslip, Janice Murfitt, Jane Suthering and Rosemary Wadey.

CONSULTANT

PAT ALBUREY is a home economist with a wide experience of preparing foods for photography, teaching cookery and creating recipes. She has written a number of cookery books including *The Harrods Book of Cakes and Desserts,* and she was the studio consultant for the Time-Life series *The Good Cook.* In addition to acting as the general consultant on this volume, she created a number of the recipes.

NUTRITION CONSULTANT

PATRICIA JUDD trained as a dietician and worked in hospital practice before returning to university to obtain her MSc and PhD degrees. Since then she has lectured in Nutrition and Dietetics at London University.

Nutritional analyses for *Fresh Ways with Cakes* were derived from McCance and Widdowson's *The Composition of Food* by A. A. Paul and D. A. T. Southgate, and other current data.

This volume is one of a series of illustrated cookery books that emphasize the preparation of healthy dishes for today's weight-conscious, nutrition-minded eaters.

Fresh Ways with Cakes

BY

THE EDITORS OF TIME-LIFE BOOKS

TIME-LIFE BOOKS/AMSTERDAM

Contents

Caraway Seed Sponge

Semolina Fruit Cake

Poppy Seed Plait

Black Cherry Chocolate Gateau

3 Small-Scale Delights 95

Raspberry and Hazelnut Roulade

4 Cakes from the Microwave 127

Cherry and Walnut Buns

The Pleasures of Baking

To many, cakes seem the epitome of nutritional frivolity — mere concentrated sugar and fat. Yet for the sweet-toothed, life without the occasional feather-light sponge, moist fruit cake or chocolate-covered morsel would be much the poorer. The 109 recipes in this volume are proof that cake can find a place in a healthy diet without overloading it with calories or sacrificing nutritional balance. A 2000-calorie daily diet can accommodate both a 175-calorie dessert and a 250-calorie snack, either of which might consist of some home-baked delight. All but seven of the recipes on the following pages fall within the 250-calorie limit, and 47 of them fall within the 175-calorie limit. But health-conscious cooks are not simply calorie counting; they want each element of the diet to provide positive benefit. These cakes also contribute to the day's intake of protein, dietary fibre, vitamins and minerals.

Above all, the cakes devised for this volume are ones in which fat — particularly saturated fat — is limited. The slices of temptation that give cakes a bad name are rich in butter and eggs and nuts, drowned in cream or chocolate. All should be consumed in moderation in a wholesome diet, since dairy products, chocolate and some nuts, notably coconut, are high in saturated fat and egg yolks are the main dietary source of cholesterol. A high level of cholesterol in the blood is strongly implicated in coronary heart disease, and blood cholesterol is raised by eating large quantities of saturated fat. Some experts believe that a diet high in cholesterol itself also helps to raise blood cholesterol.

Controlling saturated fat intake

To control the amounts of saturated fats and cholesterol in these cakes has challenged the recipe-creators' ingenuity, for the ingredients high in these undesirable fats play an important structural role. Butter and eggs make cakes moist, palatable and light: a classic technique for aerating cakes is to cream butter with sugar until the blend is fluffy with captured air bubbles.

One of the ways to cut down on saturated fat is to replace butter with a less saturated fat; polyunsaturated fats not only are not implicated in heart disease but actually seem to reduce blood cholesterol. The majority of the recipes in this volume call for polyunsaturated margarine rather than butter: many margarines, particularly the hard ones, contain nearly as much saturated fat as butter, but margarine made from sunflower oil, for instance, is predominantly polyunsaturated. The recipes in this book that use oil specify safflower, the most polyunsaturated available; if it is impossible to find, substitute sunflower, the next healthiest.

Many home-baking enthusiasts not only appreciate the health value of margarine but actually prefer it to butter. Soft margarines require less working than butter and give lighter results. On the other hand, butter confers an incomparable flavour.

The balance of health, flavour and texture can never be resolved for all time; it depends on the recipe and on each person's eating habits. Families that consume a lot of cake would be wise to cut down on butter — but if a slice of cake is a very rare treat, you may prefer to put flavour first. In most recipes, you can freely interchange margarine and butter, though a recipe that calls for butter but also contains a good deal of liquid may give too soft a result when polyunsaturated margarine is substituted. You cannot interchange oil with butter or margarine: the difference in density makes for different results and, unlike butter and margarine, oil will not incorporate air when beaten.

Butter has been limited in the cakes in this volume not only because of the risk of heart disease but also for the sake of the calorie count. Weight for weight, fat contains more than double the calories of carbohydrate or protein, so any modest diminution in the butter content of a recipe will sharply reduce calories. Substituting margarine or oil for butter does nothing for the calorie count, because margarine is as high in calories as butter, and oil still higher. But the total fat content can be reduced by finding other ways of making the cake light and moist.

Fortunately, there are a number of alternatives to creamed butter or margarine for raising a cake, all of which this volume has explored. One is a combination of eggs and sugar whisked over heat to incorporate air: *genoise*, the low-fat sponge leavened in this manner, is the foundation of many assembled creations in Chapters 2 and 3. The *genoise* mixture does contain some saturated fat from egg yolks, but very much less than a sponge based on creamed butter. The *genoise* mixture is also high in cholesterol, but dietary cholesterol is probably of less concern nutritionally than saturated fat, which raises blood cholesterol indirectly: four medium-sized eggs provide less than a gram of cholesterol, whereas the same weight of butter provides 98 g of saturated fat.

Another alternative to using creamed butter for leavening is to rely on yeast, a microscopic organism that produces carbon dioxide gas as a by-product of its metabolism. A third ploy is to use a chemical leavener such as bicarbonate of soda or baking powder. Bicarbonate of soda is an alkali that releases carbon dioxide when moistened; it is most effective if an acid is present, and most cake recipes using bicarbonate of soda include an acidic substance such as treacle, buttermilk or even vinegar. Baking powder works in a similar way but since it contains its own acid it does not need such additions. Many of the recipes in this volume rely on a mixture of leavening methods: a modest amount of creamed butter or margarine, for example, aided by a little baking powder.

Because they lack large quantities of fat, the cakes would be dry were precautions not taken. But the recipes solve the problem of dryness with many alternative moistening agents, ranging from fresh orange juice to courgettes, from tea to rum.

Novel sweeteners

While limiting fat is the prime strategy for controlling the calorie count, limiting sugar is also a help. Of course a cake needs sweetness — that is part of its beguilement — but everyone can adjust to a shade less. This volume trains the palate gently in new ways, in some recipes by cutting down a little on quantities of sugar, elsewhere by offering replacements for the white sugar traditionally poured into cakes. Sometimes the replacements provide extra flavour, sometimes fewer calories, and sometimes valuable nutrients in addition to calories.

Many of the recipes use brown instead of white sugar; brown sugar — whether dark or light, demerara crystals or sticky muscovado — has all the calories of white sugar, and negligible other nutrients, but its distinctive flavour makes a positive contribution to a cake and renders sweetness less important. One warning, however: brown sugar, because of its moisture content, is often lumpy and needs sifting before mixing with other ingredients. Black treacle and molasses, by-products of sugar refining, have less sweetness but even more flavour and also a notable nutritional value: 10 g of black treacle or molasses — a reasonable helping incorporated into a slice of cake — contain 15 per cent of a person's daily iron requirements and 5 per cent of his or her calcium needs.

Many recipes in this volume use honey alongside or instead of sugar, and a few recipes rely entirely on dried fruits for sweetness. Fructose, the sugar in fruit and honey, has, weight for weight, the same number of calories as cane or beet sugar, but one and a half times the sweetening power. Recipes that depend on honey, fruit or powdered fructose for sweetness can thus contribute fewer calories while achieving the same sweetness. Dried fruits provide iron and fibre in addition to their sweetness. Honey possesses virtually no nutritional edge over sugar but it has a different advantage: it absorbs vapour from the air, so a cake that contains it becomes moister with keeping. But honey gives a heavier result than sugar, so it is not always suitable as a substitute.

The value of flour

Flour contributes a varying proportion — up to 50 per cent in some recipes — of the calories in these cakes. Nutritionists consider flour a far better source of calories than sugar, because flour consists mainly of complex carbohydrates — chains of simple sugars which are digested more slowly than pure sugar, to satisfy hunger and provide energy for longer. Moreover, flour offers additional nutrients: about 10 per cent of wheat flour is protein, and flour is also rich in iron and the B vitamins. White flour — milled from the inner layers of the wheat grain — contains a small amount of bran, which provides dietary fibre; wholemeal flour, milled from the entire grain, contains more than double the amount of bran. Brown flour contains some of the grain's outer layer and is intermediate in fibre content between white and wholemeal flours. (When using wholemeal and brown flours, note that, unlike plain flour, they do not need sifting before being combined with the other cake ingredients: they never form lumps in the bag. However, the best way to ensure an even distribution of a raising agent or a ground or powdered spice throughout a cake is to sift it with the flour, whether or not the flour itself needs sifting.)

Some manufacturers stress that their white flour is unbleached; in fact, most of the flour sold nowadays is unbleached, whether it proclaims so or not. In this volume, plain flour is the term used for unbleached white flour.

Recipes for cakes leavened with yeast often — though not always — specify strong flour, whether plain or wholemeal; the high proportion of protein in strong flour forms a sturdy lattice

The Key to Better Eating

Healthy Home Cooking addresses the concerns of today's weight-conscious, health-minded cooks with recipes that take into account guidelines set by nutritionists. The secret to eating well, of course, has to do with maintaining a balance of foods in the diet. The recipes should therefore be used thoughtfully, in the context of a day's eating. To make the choice easier, this book, offers an analysis of the nutrients in each recipe, as on the right. The analysis is for a single small cake or a single slice of a large cake. The counts that are given for calories, protein, cholesterol, total fat, saturated fat and sodium are approximate.

Interpreting the chart

The chart below gives dietary guidelines for healthy men, women and children. Recommended figures vary from country to country, but the principles are the same everywhere. Here, the average daily amounts of calories and protein are from a report by the U.K. Department of Health and Social Security; the maximum advisable daily intake of fat is based on guidelines given by the National

Calories **215**
Protein **4g**
Cholesterol **45mg**
Total fat **6g**
Saturated fat **3g**
Sodium **35mg**

Advisory Committee on Nutrition Education (NACNE); those for cholesterol and sodium are based on upper limits suggested by the World Health Organization.

The volumes in the Healthy Home Cooking series do not purport to be diet books, nor do they focus on health foods. Rather, they express a commonsense approach to cooking that uses salt, sugar, cream, butter and oil in moderation while employing other ingredients that also provide flavour and satisfaction. In these cake recipes, spices, fruits, peels, juices, spirits and vegetables are all used towards this end.

In this volume, a conscious effort has been made to limit the cakes to 250 calories per serving — the average comes to about 195 — and to restrict the amount of total fat

and saturated fat to 10 and 5 g per helping respectively. Occasionally, in the interest of taste, texture or even the successful cooking of a cake, the amount of sugar or fat has been increased. When a cake recipe exceeds the 250-calorie limit, the cook should cut back a little elsewhere in the daily menu.

The recipes make few unusual demands. Naturally they call for fresh ingredients, offering substitutes when these are unavailable. (Only the original ingredient is calculated in the nutrient analysis, however.) Most of the ingredients can be found in any well-stocked supermarket. Any that may seem unfamiliar are described in a glossary on pages 140 and 141. In order to help the cook master new techniques, how-to photographs appear wherever appropriate.

About cooking times

Because the recipes emphasise fresh foods, they may take a bit longer to prepare than dishes that call for packaged products, but the payoff in flavour, and often in nutrition, should compensate for the little extra time involved. To help the cook plan ahead, Healthy Home Cooking provides "working" and "total" times for each cake.

Working time denotes the minutes actively spent on preparation; since no two cooks work at exactly the same speed, it is, of course, approximate. Total time includes any soaking or chilling specified in the recipe, and it includes unattended cooking time; again, because of the variations in ovens and cake tins, the cooking times given can only be an average. Total time also includes the minutes — or, more often, hours — that the cake takes to cool to room temperature. (Cooling times can vary according to the temperature of the kitchen by an hour or more.) A few cakes are not ready to slice even after they have cooled; any further resting period to knit the cake's structure is likewise included in total time.

Recommended Dietary Guidelines

		Average Daily Intake		Maximum Daily Intake			
		CALORIES	PROTEIN grams	CHOLESTEROL milligrams	TOTAL FAT grams	SATURATED FAT grams	SODIUM milligrams
Females	7-8	1900	47	300	80	32	2000*
	9-11	2050	51	300	77	35	2000
	12-17	2150	53	300	81	36	2000
	18-54	2150	54	300	81	36	2000
	54-74	1900	47	300	72	32	2000
Males	7-8	1980	49	300	80	33	2000
	9-11	2280	57	300	77	38	2000
	12-14	2640	66	300	99	44	2000
	15-17	2880	72	300	108	48	2000
	18-34	2900	72	300	109	48	2000
	35-64	2750	69	300	104	35	2000
	65-74	2400	60	300	91	40	2000

(or 5g salt)

that traps the bubbles of carbon dioxide very effectively. The result is a well risen, open-textured cake.

This volume does not subscribe to the view that wholemeal flour is invariably better than white. To be sure, it is richer in dietary fibre and some nutrients, and many people prefer its more robust flavour. On those counts, it has won a prominent place in the book. On the other hand, wholemeal flour makes for a heavier texture and a rougher appearance. For some cakes, it is simply not appropriate: wholemeal madeleines would lose their delicacy, wholemeal angel cake would be earthbound. In this volume, wholemeal flour has been used only in recipes that benefit from it. If you wish to make judicious substitutions in other recipes, add an extra ½ teaspoon of baking powder per 125 g (4 oz) of wholemeal flour.

Embellishing the exterior

Hundreds of the calories in traditional cakes come from the outside — in frostings, cream layers, butter icings. Cakes must look beautiful and festive, yet good looks need not mean dietary extravagance. This volume offers myriad ideas for decoration light in calories and fat. Instead of a thick, solid layer, icing appears as a random dribble or a lattice of piped lines. Cream is replaced with a low-fat soft cheese which provides a real nutritional benefit in the shape of protein and calcium. Hazelnut marzipan sometimes appears in place of the more fattening almond version. The jam specified for fillings is without added sugar; such jam is usually sweetened with concentrated apple juice. If you prefer, you can use reduced-sugar jam, which still offers a saving in the number of calories.

Fruit, with its glowing colours and luscious contours, provides an endless source of decorative possibilities at minimal calorific expense. Because fresh fruit does not keep well once washed and sliced, it is advisable when decorating with fruit to do so at the last possible minute.

The majority of the recipes in the four chapters that follow are completely original. Some, however, are reformed versions of traditional favourites. The rum babas on page 110, for example, made with a modest amount of butter and a light syrup, account for 175 calories and 2 g of saturated fat each, while the standard version, laden with butter and sugar, provides in the region of 550 calories and 8 g of saturated fat each. The Yule log on page 87, made from a chocolate-flavoured batter filled with chestnuts, supplies again only 175 calories and 2 g of saturated fat per slice, while a slice of a more traditional version smothered in chocolate butter icing would give some 500 calories and about 15 g of saturated fat.

Like all cake recipes, those in this book rely on meticulous measurement and careful timing. A cake is not like a casserole,

which can be varied according to the cook's whim with another splash of wine, a few more carrots. Substitutions are possible in cake recipes, but within limits that do not affect the consistency and rising capacity of the finished product. In many of the recipes alternatives are offered that do succeed.

Baking requires the cook to stay alert, since cooking times for cakes are affected by the temperature of the raw ingredients and the material of the tin. Cooking times can also vary widely from oven to oven. But if you have a fan-assisted oven, which circulates heat more quickly than a conventional oven, it is usually better to keep to the recommended cooking time and reduce the oven temperature by up to 40°C (75°F); follow the manufacturer's guidelines scrupulously.

Though a few cakes, particularly the breadlike ones, are at their most delicious served warm, thorough cooling is as crucial for success with most cakes as correctly judged cooking times. A cake cut before it has cooled completely to room temperature develops a hard crust on the cut surface; a fruit cake cut while still warm will not be thoroughly bonded and may disintegrate. On a warm cake, icing will not set and a cream or cheese topping will melt. Cooling times range from a few minutes for small cakes and 30 minutes for a sponge sandwich to approximately 2 hours for a large plain cake and 4 hours for a heavy fruit cake.

Many of the cakes in this volume are photographed with beverages, but the pictures are not intended to limit your choice of accompaniment. Provided it is not extremely sugary — and few of these cakes are — a cake served as a dessert may be enjoyed with a glass of sweet wine. To accompany a cake served as a mid-morning or mid-afternoon snack, coffee, tea and tisanes serve admirably; fruit juices make a refreshing alternative, with the added benefit of vitamin C.

As a prelude to the recipes, this volume summarizes some of the background knowledge and the techniques that benefit the health-conscious baker. First of all, the chart on pages 10 and 11 provides key nutritional data on common cake ingredients. You can compare the nutritional profiles of, say, cream and yogurt, sugar and molasses, fresh and dried apricots. If you are thinking of substituting one type of nut for another or adding a garnish of fruit, you can see the consequences of your choice.

Pages 12 and 13 concentrate on basic skills — various ways of getting air into a batter and of lining cake tins. The next six pages offer a range of low-calorie finishing touches, from fruit purées and pastry cream variations to piped soft cheese and sugared rose petals. They are designed to multiply many-fold the number of healthy cakes you can create, by enabling you to devise your own variations on the decorative ideas offered in the recipes. All cakes — healthy ones included — are primarily for pleasure; with the skills that you learn here, you will find the pleasures of creation rivalling those of consumption.

*Recommended daily intake

Dairy Products	CALORIES *1900-2900	PROTEIN *47-72 g	CHOLESTEROL *max. 300 mg	TOTAL FAT *max. 72-109 g	SATURATED FAT *max. 32-48 g	SODIUM *max. 2000 mg
		g	mg	g	g	mg
Skimmed milk	33	3	tr	tr	tr	50
Cottage cheese	95	14	15	4	2	450
Medium-fat curd cheese	182	10	10	12	7	375
Fromage frais	110	7	tr	8	5	tr
Quark	90	17	0	1	tr	35
Greek yogurt	135	6	10	10	6	75
Plain low-fat yogurt	50	5	10	1	tr	75
Buttermilk	35	4	tr	tr	tr	130
Double cream	450	2	140	48	29	25
Fat and Eggs						
Unsalted butter	740	tr	230	82	49	10
Polyunsaturated margarine	730	tr	tr	81	20	800
Safflower oil	900	tr	tr	100	10	tr
Eggs *(1 egg weighs about 50 g)*	150	12	450	11	3	140
Egg yolks	340	16	1260	31	10	50
Egg whites	35	9	0	tr	0	190

Fruits and Vegetables	CALORIES *1900-2900	PROTEIN *47-72 g	CHOLESTEROL *max. 300 mg	TOTAL FAT *max. 72-109 g	SATURATED FAT *max. 32-48 g	SODIUM *max. 2000 mg
		g	mg	g	g	mg
Apples	45	tr	0	0	0	tr
Apricots	30	tr	0	0	0	tr
Bananas	80	1	0	0	0	tr
Dates	165	1	0	tr	0	tr
Figs	40	1	0	0	0	tr
Grapes	60	tr	0	0	0	tr
Lemons	15	tr	0	0	0	tr
Oranges	35	tr	0	0	0	tr
Pineapple	45	tr	0	0	0	tr
Raspberries and strawberries	25	tr	0	0	0	tr
Dried apricots	180	5	0	0	0	55
Currants	245	2	0	0	0	20
Raisins	245	1	0	0	0	50
Sultanas	250	2	0	0	0	50
Carrots	25	1	0	tr	0	95
Courgettes and pumpkin	15	tr	0	tr	0	tr

The figures refer to 100 g (3½ oz) of raw ingredient, the edible part only, fresh unless stated.

A dash indicates that no information was available.

tr indicates that a trace is known to be present.

The figures given should be taken as a guide only; the composition of many foods can vary.

Sultanas
Calories **250**
Protein **2g**
Cholesterol **0mg**
Total fat **0g**
Saturated fat **0g**
Sodium **50mg**

Safflower oil
Calories **900**
Protein **trace**
Cholesterol **trace**
Total fat **100g**
Saturated fat **10g**
Sodium **trace**

Grapes
Calories **60**
Protein **trace**
Cholesterol **0mg**
Total fat **0g**
Saturated fat **0g**
Sodium **trace**

Unsalted butter
Calories **740**
Protein **trace**
Cholesterol **230mg**
Total fat **82g**
Saturated fat **49g**
Sodium **10mg**

	CALORIES *1900-2900	PROTEIN *47-72 g	CHOLESTEROL *max. 300 mg	TOTAL FAT *max. 72-109 g	SATURATED FAT *max. 32-48 g	SODIUM *max. 2000 mg
		g	mg	g	g	mg
Nuts and Seeds						
Almonds	565	17	0	54	4	5
Chestnuts	170	2	0	3	tr	10
Desiccated coconut	605	6	0	62	30	30
Hazelnuts	380	8	0	36	3	tr
Pine-nuts	620	35	0	51	–	50
Pistachio nuts	625	20	0	54	–	tr
Walnuts	525	11	0	52	6	tr
Sesame seeds	580	17	0	53	7	60
Sunflower seeds	490	17	0	33	–	30

	CALORIES *1900-2900	PROTEIN *47-72 g	CHOLESTEROL *max. 300 mg	TOTAL FAT *max. 72-109 g	SATURATED FAT *max. 32-48 g	SODIUM *max. 2000 mg
		g	mg	g	g	mg
Flours and Raising Agents						
Plain flour	340	11	0	1	tr	tr
Wholemeal flour	320	13	0	2	tr	tr
Cornflour	355	tr	0	tr	tr	50
Oatmeal	400	12	0	9	2	35
Baking powder	160	5	0	tr	0	11800
Bicarbonate of soda	0	0	0	0	0	27380
Sweeteners and Flavourings						
White sugar	395	tr	0	0	0	0
Demerara sugar	395	tr	0	0	0	5
Fructose	375	tr	0	0	0	0
Honey	280	tr	0	0	0	10
Molasses	215	tr	0	0	0	95
Jam (without added sugar)	110	tr	0	0	0	10
Cocoa powder	310	19	0	22	13	950
Plain chocolate	525	5	0	30	18	10

Nutrients in Cake Ingredients

Honey
Calories **280**
Protein **trace**
Cholesterol **0mg**
Total fat **0g**
Saturated fat **0g**
Sodium **10mg**

Plain low-fat yogurt
Calories **50**
Protein **5g**
Cholesterol **10mg**
Total fat **1g**
Saturated fat **trace**
Sodium trace **75mg**

Double cream
Calories **450**
Protein **2g**
Cholesterol **140mg**
Total fat **48g**
Saturated fat **29g**
Sodium trace **25mg**

Demerara sugar
Calories **395**
Protein **trace**
Cholesterol **0mg**
Total fat **0g**
Saturated fat **0g**
Sodium **5mg**

Airy Consistencies

One essential ingredient in virtually all cakes — although it does not show up in the nutrient charts — is air. This page covers three techniques that introduce air into a mixture and the consistency that you should aim for in each case.

When vigorously whisked, egg white captures air bubbles and puffs up to many times its original volume. Whether it is to be folded into a cake batter or whisked with sugar to create meringue, it should be stiff enough to hold its shape *(left)*. Yolks or whole eggs whisked over heat with sugar enfold air and become the basis of a feather-light sponge. Whisking must continue until a trail of mixture falling from the whisk forms a glossy ribbon *(below, left)*. The airy foundation of many sponges and fruit cakes is butter or margarine, beaten with sugar until its colour changes to a pale shade of cream *(below)*.

Stiffly Whisked Egg White

WHISKING WHITES. Separate eggs carefully: a trace of yolk will hinder the whites from mounting. Put the whites in a large bowl — preferably made of copper, which reacts chemically with the whites to strengthen the air bubbles. Using a balloon whisk, whisk them with a figure-of-eight motion until they begin to foam. Changing to a circular action, whisk until the whites, when lifted on the whisk, hold a peak without the tip drooping.

Eggs and Sugar Whisked Over Heat

1 *WHISKING OVER HOT WATER. Place eggs and sugar in a large bowl and set it over a pan of simmering water. Whisk with a hand or electric whisk for 5 to 10 minutes. The mixture will grow thick and pale.*

2 *FORMING A TRAIL. Remove the bowl from the heat. Continue to whisk for 5 to 10 minutes, until the mixture is cool and will fall from the whisk to form a trail that lasts for at least 10 seconds.*

Butter and Sugar Beaten to a Cream

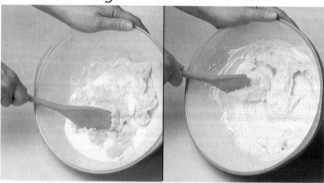

CREAMING WITH A WOODEN SPOON. Bring butter to room temperature; polyunsaturated margarine is softer and can be creamed while cool. Place margarine or — as here — butter in a large mixing bowl. Hold the bowl at an angle and use a wooden spoon or an electric mixer to beat the butter until it is soft (above, left). Beat in caster sugar — here, an equal weight is used. Continue to beat until the mixture is fluffy and virtually white.

Lining Tins for Flawless Results

A Disc for a Shallow Tin

DUSTING WITH FLOUR. Brush the inside of the tin with melted fat. Cut a circle of paper to fit the base of the tin and press it into position. If, as here, you use greaseproof paper, brush with fat, spoon in a little flour and rotate the tin to distribute it evenly. Tip away the excess.

Two Layers for a Deep Tin

LINING THE SIDES. Cut two parchment paper discs to fit the base. Cut two strips for the sides, adding an extra 4 cm (2 inches) in height. Fold a 2 cm (1 inch) hem along the strips and snip it. Grease the tin. Insert one disc, then the side strips. Grease the first disc; add the second.

Moulds for small cakes need no more preparation than a film of butter or margarine and perhaps a dusting with flour: the flour browns to give the cake a light crust. But tins for large cakes must be lined with paper to help the cooked cake slip out without breaking.

This page shows how to prepare linings for a shallow sandwich tin *(far left)*, a deep round cake tin *(left)* and a rectangular tin *(below)*. For a shallow tin, whether round or rectangular, a base lining is adequate. To help turn out a deep cake, the sides of the tin are lined as well. For a long-cooking cake, such as a fruit cake, the double lining shown on the deep round tin will prevent scorching.

Parchment paper with a silicone coating to prevent sticking is the best material for lining cake tins. In place of parchment paper you can use well-greased greaseproof paper. Parchment paper does not usually need greasing, though a light coating of fat is recommended in a few recipes for mixtures that are particularly liable to stick.

A Tailored Lining for a Rectangular Tin

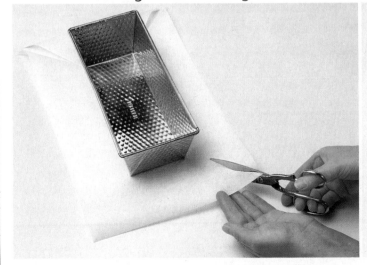

1 *CUTTING NEAT CORNERS. Cut a sheet of non-stick parchment paper large enough to cover the base and sides of the tin. Place the tin in the centre of the sheet. Cut a straight diagonal line from each corner of the paper to the nearest corner of the tin (above).*

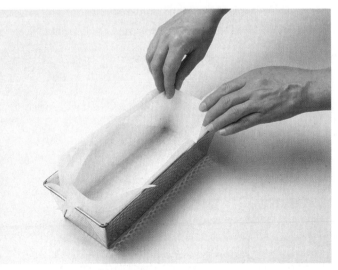

2 *FITTING THE PAPER. Grease the inside of the tin with melted fat. Insert the paper into the tin, and press it firmly against the base and sides. Overlap the corner flaps, lightly greasing their undersides so that the pairs of flaps adhere and lie flat.*

Techniques for Preparing Fruit

The rich colours and fresh flavours of fruits, together with their low calorie content and total lack of fat, make them invaluable for filling and decorating healthy cakes.

Some fruits, such as strawberries and raspberries, can be used as decoration just as they are, but citrus fruits must be rid of peel and pith *(right)*, while peaches and apricots need light cooking to loosen their skins and soften them *(below, right)*.

For filling or topping sponges, lemon curd or fresh fruit purées thickened with arrowroot *(opposite page)* make perfect alternatives to jam. Below appear two methods of puréeing fruits, suitable for soft fruits and firm fruits respectively. Apples and pears, however, demand a third technique. They should be peeled, sliced and cooked gently in a heavy-bottomed saucepan with a few tablespoons of water and a little sugar — about 90 g (3 oz) per 500 g (1 lb) of fruit — until they become soft and fluffy. After draining in a nylon sieve to remove excess juice, the resulting purée needs no thickening with arrowroot.

Segmenting an Orange

1 *REMOVING THE PEEL. Using a sharp knife, slice off the peel at both ends of the orange. Stand the fruit on a flat end and slice downwards to remove the peel and pith in vertical strips. This technique of cutting away peel and pith together ensures that every trace of pith is removed.*

2 *CUTTING OUT THE SEGMENTS. Working over a bowl to catch the juice, hold the orange in one hand and slice between flesh and membrane to remove each segment. The segments will now make a fresh and appealing cake decoration.*

Two Ways of Puréeing

SIEVING SOFT FRUITS. To purée raspberries, blackberries or — as here — strawberries, put the fruit in a nylon sieve set over a bowl. Using a wooden pestle, push the fruit through the sieve. Before sieving apricots, peaches, plums and currants, cook them first for a few minutes in a heavy-bottomed saucepan with a little sugar — 60 to 125 g (2 to 4 oz) per 500 g (1 lb) of fruit.

BLENDING FIRM FRUITS. Purée firm fruits such as mangoes, papaya or — as here — pineapple in a blender or food processor. Peel and core the pineapple and cut the flesh into chunks. Put the pineapple in the food processor or blender, and process the fruit in short bursts.

Removing Skins

POACHING AND SKINNING. Halve and stone plums or — as here — apricots. Simmer the halves in water until tender — 3 to 7 minutes. Drain them on a drum sieve, and pull off the skins. With peaches and nectarines, immerse the whole fruit in boiling water for 2 minutes. Drain, skin, halve and stone the fruit. Poach the halves until tender — 5 to 15 minutes.

Thickened Fruit Purée

WITH THE EXCEPTION OF APPLE PURÉE, MOST FRUIT PURÉES NEED TO BE THICKENED BEFORE THEY CAN BE USED AS CAKE FILLINGS OR TOPPINGS, SO THAT THEY DO NOT OOZE OUT OR RUN OFF THE FINISHED CAKE. WHEN THICKENED WITH ARROWROOT THEY BECOME CLEAR AND SPARKLING, WITH A SOFT, JELLY-LIKE CONSISTENCY.

Makes ¼ litre (8 fl oz)
Working time: about 10 minutes
Total time: about 1 hour and 30 minutes

¼ litre	fresh fruit purée (opposite)	8 fl oz
1 tbsp	arrowroot	1 tbsp
30 g	caster sugar	1 oz

Put the fruit purée in a small saucepan. Blend the arrowroot with 1 tablespoon of cold water, then stir it into the purée. Bring the purée to the boil, stirring continuously; boil until the mixture thickens and clears. Continue to cook the purée over a low heat for 3 to 4 minutes, until there is no trace of any uncooked arrowroot. Stir in the sugar.

Pour the purée into a small bowl and cover the surface closely with plastic film, to prevent a skin from forming. Allow the thickened purée to cool, then refrigerate it until it is set and thoroughly chilled.

EDITOR'S NOTE: About 250 g (8 oz) of prepared fresh fruit will yield ¼ litre (8 fl oz) of purée.

Lemon Curd

Makes 500 g (1 lb)
Working time: about 40 minutes
Total time: about 4 hours

2	lemons, rind finely grated, juice squeezed and strained	2
90 g	polyunsaturated margarine	3 oz
125 g	caster sugar	4 oz
3	eggs, lightly whisked	3

Put the lemon rind and juice, margarine and sugar in a mixing bowl. Strain the eggs through a sieve into the bowl. Place the bowl over a saucepan of gently simmering water, making sure that the bottom of the bowl does not touch the water. Stir the mixture continuously over the heat (Step 2, below) until it becomes thick enough to leave a trail when the spoon is lifted — 20 to 25 minutes. Alternatively, put the bowl in a microwave oven and cook the lemon curd on high for 3 minutes, stirring every 30 seconds with a wire whisk.

Immediately the mixture thickens, transfer it to a clean, warm jar. Allow the lemon curd to cool, then refrigerate it. When the lemon curd is cold, cover the jar with a clean lid or a cellophane disc secured with a rubber band. Keep the jar refrigerated and use the lemon curd within two weeks.

Making Lemon Curd

1 COMBINING THE INGREDIENTS. Put caster sugar in a bowl with margarine, lemon rind and juice (see recipe above). Lightly whisk eggs in another bowl. Add the whisked eggs to the other ingredients, pouring them through a nylon sieve to remove any white threads.

2 THICKENING THE CURD. Stand the bowl over a pan of gently simmering water. So that the eggs do not cook too quickly and coagulate in lumps, make sure that the bottom of the bowl does not touch the water. Cook the curd, stirring constantly, for about 20 to 25 minutes.

3 STORING THE CURD. When the curd begins to thicken and will hold a ribbon trail, warm a clean glass jar to prevent it from cracking, then spoon in the curd and leave it to cool completely. (It will thicken further as it cools.) Cover the container with a lid and store it in the refrigerator.

Pastry Cream Variations

PASTRY CREAM OR *CRÈME PÂTISSIÈRE* IS A CUSTARD USED FOR FILLING AND DECORATING CAKES; IT IS TRADITIONALLY ENRICHED WITH NUMEROUS EGG YOLKS AND THICKENED WITH FLOUR. THIS VERSION IS ENRICHED ONLY WITH A LITTLE GREEK YOGURT; CORNFLOUR REPLACES FLOUR BECAUSE, IN THE ABSENCE OF EGG YOLKS, CORNFLOUR IS EASIER TO BLEND WITH THE OTHER INGREDIENTS. THE EGG WHITE LIGHTENS THE MIXTURE BUT IS NOT ESSENTIAL. THE BASIC PASTRY CREAM RECIPE CAN BE ENLIVENED WITH THE ADDITION OF A VARIETY OF FLAVOURINGS.

Makes 60 cl (1 pint)
Working time: about 20 minutes
Total time: about 4 hours

60 g	cornflour	2 oz
60 g	caster sugar	2 oz
60 cl	skimmed milk	1 pint
1 tsp	pure vanilla extract	1 tsp
1	egg white (optional)	1
60 g	thick Greek yogurt	2 oz

Blend the cornflour in a bowl with the sugar and 2 tablespoons of the milk. Pour the remaining milk into a saucepan and bring it to the boil. Pour the boiling milk on to the blended cornflour, stirring continuously. Pour the custard back into the saucepan and cook over a low heat, stirring, for 6 to 8 minutes until every trace of raw cornflour has gone. Beat in the vanilla extract. Strain the custard through a nylon sieve into a clean bowl and cover the surface closely with plastic film to prevent a skin from forming. Allow the pastry cream to cool, then refrigerate it for 2 to 3 hours, or overnight, until it is completely cold.

Whisk the cold custard until it is very smooth. Whisk the egg white until it forms soft peaks. Fold the yogurt into the custard, then gradually fold in the egg white. Cover the bowl and return the pastry cream to the refrigerator to chill thoroughly.

Liqueur-flavoured pastry cream. Stir 4 tablespoons of brandy, rum or a liqueur such as kirsch into the custard at the same time as the vanilla extract.

Orange-flavoured pastry cream. Add the grated rind of 2 oranges to the cold milk in the saucepan. In place of the vanilla extract, add 2 tablespoons of Grand Marnier.

Coffee-flavoured pastry cream. Stir 2 tablespoons of very strong black coffee into the custard with the vanilla extract.

Chocolate-flavoured pastry cream. Add 2 tablespoons of cocoa powder to the initial blend of cornflour, sugar and milk.

Almond pastry cream. Beat 60 g (2 oz) of ground almonds and 3 drops of almond extract into the custard at the same time as the Greek yogurt.

Essential Piping Skills

An edge of piped shells or lattice of piped lines adds a polished finish to an otherwise simple cake. Since piping makes small amounts of topping go further, it is often used in this volume for distributing cream, glacé icing and chocolate. You can also pipe low-fat soft cheese and a low-calorie adaptation of classic pastry cream *(box, left)*. When piped, a low-fat cheese gives crisp outlines; pastry cream, especially when lightened with egg white, has softer contours.

Dribbling fine lines of icing or chocolate is best accomplished with a home-made greaseproof paper icing bag *(far right)*. For piping cream, pastry cream or soft cheese, use a nylon bag fitted with a nozzle — a star nozzle is the most versatile. The photographs on the right show how to fill a bag correctly. Below appear three designs that you can achieve with the star nozzle. If you have not piped before, it is best to practise on a work surface or on an upturned plate before embellishing the cake.

Three Basic Patterns

Fit a piping bag with a medium star nozzle and fill the bag (right, above): here, soft cheese is used. Grasp the bag with one hand at the top to squeeze, and the other hand near the nozzle to direct it. To pipe stars, hold the piping bag vertical, just above the work surface. Squeeze the piping bag gently; when the star reaches the size you want, stop squeezing and lift the bag away sharply. To pipe a straight line, hold the bag at an angle to the work surface, and only just above it. Pipe towards yourself, keeping an even pressure on the bag. To finish, lower the nozzle and pull the bag sharply to one side. To pipe shells, hold the bag at an angle, close to the work surface. Squeeze a small mound, then raise the bag. Reduce the pressure; lower the bag as you bring it towards you. Repeat the sequence to create a series of overlapping shells.

A ROW OF STARS

A FLUTED LINE

A STRING OF SHELLS

Making an Icing Bag

Preparing to Pipe

1 FORMING A CONE. *Cut a square from a sheet of greaseproof paper, then cut it in half diagonally. Using one triangle only, bring one corner of the long side to meet the right-angle corner, turning the first corner over as you move it.*

1 FILLING THE BAG. *Push a nozzle into position in a piping bag. Fold the top of the bag back and hold the bag by the neck thus formed. Fill the bag no more than three quarters full with the mixture — here, pastry cream.*

2 EXCLUDING AIR. *Supporting the bag loosely with one hand, twist the top of the bag with the other. This action will squeeze out any air pockets and leave the bag ready for piping.*

2 COMPLETING THE CONE. *Keeping the first corner in position, bring the remaining corner over to the right-angle corner in the same way. Holding the corners in both hands, adjust them to create a perfect point at the cone's tip.*

3 SECURING THE BAG. *Fold over the corners of the triangle to prevent the cone from coming apart. Snip the tip to form a hole through which to dribble icing or chocolate. The size of the hole will determine the thickness of the dribble.*

Decorative Ideas

Some of the prettiest cake decorations are simple and low in calories. Citrus peel, cut into julienne strips *(right)*, lends colour and contrast. A sugar frosting transforms grapes or edible flower petals *(far right)* into sparkling jewels. Chocolate is high in fat and calories, but curls and rose leaves *(opposite page)* make the most of small quantities; a chocolate leaf contains a mere 18 calories.

A sprinkling of icing sugar finishes a sponge attractively and adds only about 5 calories per slice. For a patterned surface, you can mask part of the cake with card shapes or with strips of greaseproof paper *(below)* before sifting the sugar over. Or, you can brand the sugar with a red-hot skewer *(below, right)* to create caramelized stripes.

Julienne Strips

PARING AND BLANCHING. Pare thin layers of rind in long strips from an orange, a lime or — as here — a lemon. Scrape any white pith from the rind, and trim ragged edges. Cut the rind into narrow strips (above). Parboil the strips for 3 minutes, drain them and pat them dry.

Sugar-Frosted Petals

APPLYING A COATING. Beat an egg white until it lightens without foaming. Brush violets, primroses, geraniums or — as here — rose petals with the white, then dip them in caster sugar. Transfer the petals to a plate and leave them in a warm place until dry and hard. In an airtight container, they will keep for weeks.

Stencil Patterns with Icing Sugar

MASKING AREAS OF THE CAKE. Cut strips of greaseproof paper, each about 1 cm (½ inch) wide and slightly longer than the diameter of the cake. Lay them on top of the cake and sift icing sugar evenly over the surface. Lift away each strip carefully, to avoid scattering the sugar.

Heat-Branded Icing Sugar

APPLYING A RED-HOT SKEWER. Sift a thick, even layer of icing sugar over the cake. Heat a long skewer in a flame or on an electric ring, protecting your hand with a cloth if the skewer lacks a wooden handle. When the skewer is red hot, hold it against the cake. Brand the cake with parallel lines or a grid pattern, reheating the skewer if necessary.

Chocolate Curls

SCRAPING THE BLOCK. Choose soft chocolate for long curls; hard chocolate gives shorter curls. The chocolate must be at room temperature, otherwise it may not curl. Hold the block over a plate and draw a vegetable peeler along the thin edge, allowing the shavings to curl and fall free.

Chocolate Rose Leaves

1 *COATING A LEAF. Wipe some small rose leaves with kitchen paper. Break a bar of chocolate into small, even-sized pieces: 75 g (2½ oz) of chocolate yields 20 leaves. Put the chocolate on a plate and set it over a saucepan of simmering water until the chocolate melts. Holding each leaf by its stem, gently press the underside of the leaf against the chocolate. Pull the leaf across the side of the plate to remove excess chocolate.*

2 *PEELING AWAY A LEAF. Transfer the leaves, chocolate side uppermost, to a clean plate. Leave them in a cool place — but not in the refrigerator — until the chocolate has set hard. Then, starting at the stem end (above), carefully peel each natural leaf away from its chocolate counterpart.*

1 *Candied peel, sultanas, molasses and other ingredients for a moist, dark fruit cake await the cook's attentions.*

Simple Sponges & Fruit Cakes

Cakes for every day should beguile the eye and palate without requiring elaborate assembly or intricate decoration. The cakes in this chapter will grace a family meal, honour an unexpected caller or satisfy a bevy of hungry children — and although they may take several hours to bake and cool, few demand more than 30 minutes of the cook's active efforts. Ranging from a frosted orange sponge to a moist, fruit-packed Dundee cake, the recipes cater for every taste.

The airiest cakes of all, the angel food cakes, might have been invented with the health-conscious cook in mind. Lacking all fat, angel food cake is raised to prodigious heights with stiffly beaten egg whites alone. Other sponge cakes, by contrast, are aerated chiefly with fat and sugar which have been creamed to virtual whiteness. The classic sponge consists of equal weights of eggs, flour, sugar and butter or margarine, together with flavourings such as chocolate, sherry or orange rind; but in these recipes the proportion of fat is reduced and baking powder is generally enlisted to help leaven the cake.

Dense and dark, the dried fruit and nut cakes on pages 42 to 54 offer a striking contrast to the feather-light sponges. Some of the dried fruit and nut cakes, like the sponges, are raised partly with creamed fat, but a number are fatless mixtures leavened with baking powder alone; others include small proportions of fat which is rubbed into the flour with the fingers. Variety comes not just from different mixtures of vine fruits, tropical fruits, candied peels and nuts, but also from a range of flour types including malted wheat flour, dark rye flour and protein-rich soya flour.

The spice cakes, fresh fruit cakes and vegetable cakes that make up the rest of this chapter are no less diverse. For flavour and moisture, they employ a range of surprising ingredients from saffron, pineapple and banana, to pumpkins and courgettes.

Step-by-step photographs within the chapter offer guidance for specialized procedures, such as creating the poppy seed plait shown on pages 38 and 39. For basic cake-making and decorating techniques, including creaming butter and lining tins, pages 12 to 19 provide more detail than the individual recipes.

Sponge Layer Variations

THE CLASSIC SPONGE CAKE, OFTEN KNOWN AS POUND CAKE OR VICTORIA SANDWICH, CONTAINS EQUAL WEIGHTS OF EGG, FLOUR, SUGAR AND BUTTER OR MARGARINE. THIS RECIPE, WHICH REDUCES THE PROPORTION OF EGG AND RAISES THAT OF FLOUR TO GIVE A LESS RICH CAKE, CAN BE VARIED WITH DIFFERENT FLAVOURINGS, FILLINGS AND TOPPINGS.

Serves 12
Working time: about 20 minutes
Total time: about 1 hour and 30 minutes

Plain sponge with jam filling:
Calories **190**
Protein **3g**
Cholesterol **45mg**
Total fat **9g**
Saturated fat **3g**
Sodium **140mg**

125 g	polyunsaturated margarine	4 oz
140 g	caster sugar	4½ oz
150 g	plain flour	5 oz
1½ tsp	baking powder	1½ tsp
2	eggs	2
4 tsp	fresh lemon juice	4 tsp
3 tbsp	raspberry, strawberry or apricot jam without added sugar	3 tbsp

Wholemeal sponge with jam-cheese filling:
Calories **185**
Protein **3g**
Cholesterol **45mg**
Total fat **9g**
Saturated fat **3g**
Sodium **135mg**

Chocolate sponge with fromage frais filling:
Calories **180**
Protein **3g**
Cholesterol **45mg**
Total fat **10g**
Saturated fat **3g**
Sodium **135mg**

Preheat the oven to 190°C (375°F or Mark 5). Grease two 19 to 20 cm (7½ to 8 inch) sandwich tins. Line their bases with non-stick parchment paper or greaseproof paper; grease the paper. Dredge the tins with flour and shake out the surplus.

Cream the margarine with 125 g (4 oz) of the sugar in a large bowl until very pale and fluffy. Sift the flour and baking powder together into another bowl. Using a wooden spoon, beat the eggs, one at a time, into the sugar mixture, following each with 1 tablespoon of the flour. Mix in the remaining flour and the lemon juice. Divide the mixture between the two prepared tins and level the surfaces.

Bake the sponges for 20 to 25 minutes until well risen, golden-brown and just firm to the touch. Turn them out on to a wire rack and leave them with the paper still attached until they have cooled completely.

When cool, strip off the paper. Place one sponge layer on a plate, and spread it with the jam. Set the second layer on top of the first and sift the remaining sugar evenly over the cake.

Variations

1. For a richer flavour and a moister texture, make the sponge with light brown sugar in place of caster sugar.

2. For a wholemeal sponge, replace half the flour with wholemeal flour and increase the amount of baking powder by ¼ teaspoon.

3. For a lemon sponge, add the grated rind of 1 lemon.

4. For a chocolate sponge, replace 20g (¾ oz) of the flour with sifted cocoa powder and use water in place of the lemon juice.

5. For a richer filling, beat 2 tablespoons of medium-fat curd cheese into the jam.

6. Replace the jam filling with a thickened fruit purée (page 15), lemon curd (page 15), flavoured pastry cream (page 16) or 4 tablespoons of fromage frais sweetened with 1 tablespoon of icing sugar.

7. Sift 15 g (½ oz) of icing sugar over the cake in place of the caster sugar. Alternatively, lay a doily on the sponge and sift 30 g (1 oz) of icing sugar over it. Lift away the doily to reveal a pattern on the cake.

Clockwise from top: plain sponge with jam filling and caster sugar topping; wholemeal sponge with jam-cheese filling and icing sugar topping; chocolate sponge with fromage frais filling and icing sugar topping.

Frosted Orange Cake

Serves 14
Working time: about 25 minutes
Total time: about 3 hours and 30 minutes

300 g	plain flour	10 oz
2½ tsp	baking powder	2½ tsp
125 g	polyunsaturated margarine	4 oz
90 g	light brown sugar	3 oz
2	oranges, grated rind only	2
2	eggs	2
3 tbsp	fresh orange juice	3 tbsp
Orange glacé icing		
125 g	icing sugar	4 oz
3 tsp	fresh orange juice	3 tsp
½	orange, grated rind only	½

Calories **214**
Protein **3g**
Cholesterol **30mg**
Total fat **7g**
Saturated fat **2g**
Sodium **100mg**

Preheat the oven to 170°C (325°F or Mark 3). Line an 18 cm (7 inch) round cake tin with non-stick parchment paper.

Sift the flour and baking powder together into a bowl and rub in the margarine until the mixture resembles fine breadcrumbs. Stir in the sugar and orange rind. In another bowl, beat the eggs and fresh orange juice together and then mix them into the dry ingredients with a wooden spoon. Turn the batter into the prepared tin and level the top. Bake the cake for about 1 hour, until well risen and firm to the touch; a skewer inserted in the centre of the cake should come out clean. Turn the cake on to a wire rack, leave it until cool and then peel off the paper.

To make the icing, sift the icing sugar into a bowl and beat in just enough of the orange juice to give a thick coating consistency. Spread the icing over the top of the cake, allowing it to run down the sides in places. Sprinkle the icing with the grated orange rind and leave the cake until the icing has set.

Coffee Sandwich

Serves 12
Working time: about 30 minutes
Total time: about 2 hours and 15 minutes

Calories **190**			
Protein **3g**	125 g	polyunsaturated margarine	4 oz
Cholesterol **45mg**	125 g	light brown sugar	4 oz
Total fat **9g**	2	eggs	2
Saturated fat **3g**	60 g	wholemeal flour	2 oz
Sodium **160mg**	125 g	plain flour	4 oz
	1¾ tsp	baking powder	1¾ tsp
	1 tbsp	black treacle	1 tbsp
	1 tbsp	very strong black coffee	1 tbsp
	15 cl	coffee-flavoured pastry cream (page 16)	¼ pint
	2 tbsp	icing sugar	2 tbsp

Preheat the oven to 190°C (375°F or Mark 5). Grease two 20 cm (8 inch) round sandwich tins and line their bases with non-stick parchment paper.

Cream the margarine and brown sugar together in a bowl until pale and fluffy. With a wooden spoon, beat in the eggs one at a time, following each with 1 tablespoon of the wholemeal flour. Sift the plain flour with the baking powder and mix it with the remaining wholemeal flour; then add the flours to the creamed mixture, alternating them with the black treacle and coffee. Divide the batter between the prepared tins and level the tops. Cook the sponges for 20 to 25 minutes, until well risen and firm to the touch. Turn them out on to a wire rack, leave them until completely cooled and then peel off the paper.

To assemble the cake, stand one sponge layer on a serving plate and spread the coffee-flavoured pastry cream evenly over it. Cover it with the second sponge layer, then sift the icing sugar over the cake. Heat a skewer until it is red hot and use it to brand a lattice pattern on the cake (page 18). To soften the contrast between the brand marks and the rest of the surface, complete the decoration with a second, very light dusting of icing sugar.

Chiffon Cake with Raspberry-Cream Filling

CHIFFON SPONGE OBTAINS A THREEFOLD LEAVENING FROM BEATEN EGG WHITES, BAKING POWDER AND THE STEAM ESCAPING FROM A MOIST BATTER. OIL IS TRADITIONALLY USED IN THE MIXTURE; THIS RECIPE KEEPS THE PROPORTION VERY LOW.

Serves 16
Working time: about 35 minutes
Total time: about 1 hour and 20 minutes

Calories **210**
Protein **3g**
Cholesterol **45mg**
Total fat **9g**
Saturated fat **2g**
Sodium **110mg**

175 g	plain flour	6 oz
3 tsp	baking powder	3 tsp
125 g	caster sugar, plus 1 tbsp	4 oz
3 tbsp	safflower oil	3 tbsp
3	egg yolks	3
6	egg whites	6

Fruit and cream filling		
75 g	caster sugar	2½ oz
4	fresh peaches, sliced	4
2 tbsp	brandy	2 tbsp
¼ litre	whipping cream	8 fl oz
125 g	fresh raspberries	4 oz

Preheat the oven to 170°C (325°F or Mark 3). Grease two 20 cm (8 inch) round sandwich tins. Line the bases with greaseproof paper and grease the paper.

Sift the flour and baking powder into a bowl and mix in 125 g (4 oz) of the sugar. Make a well in the centre. In another bowl, whisk the oil and egg yolks with 5 tablespoons of water until well blended. Pour the egg yolk mixture into the dry ingredients and beat with a wooden spoon to create a smooth, glossy batter.

Whisk the egg whites until they are stiff but not dry. Add one third of the egg whites to the batter and fold them in using a spatula or large metal or plastic spoon. Then carefully fold in the remaining whites.

Divide the mixture equally between the two tins, and tap the tins to level the mixture. Bake the sponges in the centre of the oven, until well risen, lightly browned and springy when touched in the centre — about 20 minutes. Loosen the edges of the sponges with a palette knife, turn them out on to a wire rack and remove the paper. Leave until completely cool.

Meanwhile, prepare the filling. Put 60 g (2 oz) of the sugar and 15 cl (¼ pint) of water in a wide, shallow saucepan. Heat gently, stirring, until the sugar dissolves, then bring the water to the boil. Boil the syrup gently for 4 to 5 minutes to reduce it slightly. Simmer the peach slices in the syrup for 1 to 2 minutes, until they begin to soften. Using a slotted spoon, transfer the slices to kitchen paper to drain. Peel the slices. Stir 1 tablespoon of the brandy into the poaching syrup. Whisk the cream with the remaining sugar and brandy in a large bowl until the cream will hold soft peaks.

Set one of the sponge layers on a serving plate. Spoon half the syrup evenly over the sponge, then spread the sponge with half the whipped cream. Arrange the peach slices and raspberries on the cream. Spread the remaining cream over the fruit.

Leaving the remaining sponge upside down on the rack, spoon the remaining brandy syrup over it. Then turn it over and set it on the first layer. Sift the tablespoon of caster sugar over the cake.

EDITOR'S NOTE: *To make a chocolate chiffon cake, replace 30 g (1 oz) of the flour with cocoa powder.*

Streusel Ring

STREUSEL — "CRUMBS"IN GERMAN — IS A CRUMBLY TOPPING
COMPOSED OF FLOUR RUBBED WITH FAT AND FLAVOURINGS.

Serves 16
Working time: about 25 minutes
Total time: about 3 hours and 30 minutes

Calories **230**
Protein **3g**
Cholesterol **35mg**
Total fat **10g**
Saturated fat **4g**
Sodium **145mg**

300 g	plain flour	10 oz
2½ tsp	baking powder	2½ tsp
125 g	polyunsaturated margarine	4 oz
60 g	shredded coconut	2 oz
90 g	light brown sugar	3 oz
2	limes, grated rind only	2
2	eggs	2
2 tbsp	clear honey	2 tbsp
4 tbsp	skimmed milk	4 tbsp
Coconut streusel topping		
60 g	wholemeal flour	2 oz
30 g	polyunsaturated margarine	1 oz
30 g	demerara sugar	1 oz
1 tbsp	shredded coconut	1 tbsp

Preheat the oven to 180°C (350°F or Mark 4). Thoroughly grease a tubular springform cake tin approximately 22 cm (9 inches) in diameter.

Sift the flour and baking powder into a bowl and rub in the margarine until the mixture resembles fine breadcrumbs. Mix in the coconut, sugar and lime rind. Put the eggs, honey and milk into a small bowl and whisk them together, then beat them into the dry ingredients with a wooden spoon. Turn the batter into the prepared tin and level the top.

To make the streusel topping, put the flour into a bowl and rub in the margarine. Mix in the sugar and shredded coconut. Sprinkle the blend evenly over the top of the batter. Cook the streusel ring for about 1 hour, until well risen and firm; a skewer inserted in the centre should come out clean. Leave the cake in the tin for 5 minutes to allow it to shrink from the sides, then release the spring and turn the cake out carefully on to a wire rack to cool.

Pistachio Battenburg Cake

THE CHEQUERED BATTENBURG CAKE IS USUALLY COVERED IN ALMOND MARZIPAN; HERE, PISTACHIOS REPLACE ALMONDS, TO GIVE A MARZIPAN WITH AN UNUSUAL FLAVOUR AND A NATURAL GREEN COLOUR.

Serves 16
Working time: about 1 hour
Total time: about 14 hours

Calories **250**
Protein **3g**
Cholesterol **30mg**
Total fat **12g**
Saturated fat **2g**
Sodium **180mg**

125 g	polyunsaturated margarine	4 oz
125 g	light brown sugar	4 oz
2	eggs	2
175 g	plain flour	6 oz
1½ tsp	baking powder	1½ tsp
2 tsp	strong black coffee	2 tsp
1 tsp	cocoa powder	1 tsp
3 tbsp	apricot jam without added sugar	3 tbsp
Pistachio marzipan		
175 g	shelled pistachio nuts	6 oz
90 g	caster sugar	3 oz
90 g	icing sugar	3 oz
1 tsp	fresh lemon juice	1 tsp
1	egg white, lightly beaten	1

For the pistachio marzipan, blanch the pistachio nuts for 2 minutes in simmering water. Drain them, enfold

them in a towel and rub them to loosen their skins. Peel the kernels. Spread them out on kitchen paper for several hours to dry in a warm place.

Preheat the oven to 180°C (350°F or Mark 4). Line a rectangular tin approximately 28 by 18 by 4 cm (11 by 7 by 1½ inches) with non-stick parchment paper, making a deep pleat across the centre to divide the tin crosswise into two portions.

Using a wooden spoon, cream the margarine and brown sugar together in a large bowl until very pale and fluffy. Beat in the eggs one at a time, following each with 1 tablespoon of the flour. Sift the remaining flour and the baking powder together into the mixture and fold them in.

Transfer half of the mixture to a second bowl. Into one portion beat the coffee; into the other, beat the cocoa powder together with 2 teaspoons of water. Spoon the coffee sponge mixture into one side of the prepared tin and the chocolate mixture into the other side. Cook the sponges for 20 to 25 minutes, until they are firm to the touch. Turn them out on to a wire rack, remove the lining paper and leave them to get cold.

Meanwhile, grind the pistachios finely into a bowl, using a rotary grater or a food processor. Add the caster sugar and sift in the icing sugar. Mix in the lemon juice and enough of the beaten egg white to give a firm but pliable consistency.

Trim the sponges to the same size and cut each in half lengthwise. Spread the side of one chocolate sponge lightly with jam and press one of the coffee sponges against it. Join the other two sponges with jam in the same way. Spread jam over the top of one pair of sponges. Press the second pair down on the first, making sure that a coffee sponge is over a chocolate sponge, and a chocolate sponge is over a coffee sponge, so that the cake will have a chequerboard cross section.

Dust the pistachio marzipan with a little icing sugar and roll it out between two sheets of non-stick parchment paper. Remove the top sheet and trim the marzipan into a rectangle just large enough to enclose the sponge — about 30 by 22 cm (12 by 9 inches). Spread all four surfaces of the sponge very lightly with jam and position it in the centre of the marzipan. Wrap the marzipan evenly round the sponge, peeling back the parchment paper. Press the edges of the marzipan together so that they adhere — they are very sticky — and trim off the ends.

Stand the Battenburg cake on a serving plate and score the top of the cake with a sharp knife to give a criss-cross pattern. Pinch the top edges with a finger and thumb. Leave the Battenburg cake uncovered overnight; it will become dry enough to slice.

Chocolate Marble Cake

THIS IS A VARIATION ON THE TRADITIONAL MADEIRA CAKE: A PLAIN, DRYISH MIXTURE THAT RELIES ON BUTTER FOR FLAVOUR. HERE, TO KEEP THE SATURATED FAT LEVEL DOWN, A COMBINATION OF BUTTER AND POLYUNSATURATED MARGARINE IS USED. THE WRINKLED SURFACE OF THE MARBLE CAKE IS TYPICAL OF ALL MADEIRA CAKES AND RESULTS FROM THE DRYNESS OF THE MIXTURE.

Serves 20
Working time: about 20 minutes
Total time: about 3 hours

Calories **215**
Protein **3g**
Cholesterol **60mg**
Total fat **13g**
Saturated fat **5g**
Sodium **145mg**

350 g	plain flour	12 oz
3 tsp	baking powder	3 tsp
175 g	caster sugar	6 oz
150 g	unsalted butter	5 oz
125 g	polyunsaturated margarine	4 oz
4	eggs	4
1½ tbsp	cocoa powder	1½ tbsp

Preheat the oven to 170°C (325°F or Mark 3). Grease a 20 cm (8 inch) round cake tin. Line the tin with greaseproof paper and grease the paper.

Sift the flour and baking powder into a mixing bowl. Add the sugar, butter, margarine and eggs. Mix them together, then beat the batter with a wooden spoon for 2 to 3 minutes until it is smooth and glossy. Transfer half of the batter to another bowl.

Dissolve the cocoa in 3 tablespoons of boiling water and blend the paste until it is smooth. Add the cocoa mixture to one of the bowls of batter and stir to incorporate it. Then transfer alternate spoonfuls of plain and chocolate batter to the prepared cake tin. Tap the tin to level the batter and swirl a skewer through it to create a marbled effect.

Bake the cake in the centre of the oven, until risen, lightly browned and springy when touched in the centre — 50 to 55 minutes. Loosen the edges with a small palette knife, turn the cake out of the tin on to a wire rack and remove the lining paper. Leave the cake to cool completely.

EDITOR'S NOTE: *To vary the chocolate marble cake, add 1 teaspoon of grated orange rind to the plain batter. To make a coffee marble cake, replace the dissolved cocoa with 3 tablespoons of very strong black coffee.*

Apricot and Pine-Nut Roll

THIS CAKE IS FILLED AND ROLLED AS SOON AS IT COMES OUT OF THE
OVEN, WHILE THE SPONGE IS STILL FLEXIBLE, SO THE FILLING MUST
BE PREPARED BEFORE THE SPONGE IS COOKED.

Serves 12
Working time: about 40 minutes
Total time: about 1 hour and 15 minutes

Calories **145**
Protein **5g**
Cholesterol **35mg**
Total fat **5g**
Saturated fat **0g**
Sodium **50mg**

175 g	dried apricots	6 oz
30 cl	fresh orange juice	½ pint
2 tbsp	plain low-fat yogurt	2 tbsp
2	eggs	2
60 g	light brown sugar	2 oz
60 g	brown flour	2 oz
½ tsp	baking powder	½ tsp
90 g	pine-nuts, finely ground	3 oz
2	egg whites	2
1 tbsp	caster sugar	1 tbsp

Preheat the oven to 180°C (350°F or Mark 4). Grease a
32 by 22 cm (13 by 9 inch) Swiss roll tin. Line it with
greaseproof paper and grease the paper.

Put the apricots and orange juice in a saucepan.
Bring the juice to the boil and simmer the apricots for
about 10 minutes, until they are tender and have absorbed nearly all the orange juice. Leave the fruit to
cool for 10 minutes, then purée it with the yogurt in a
blender or food processor. Set aside.

Put the eggs and brown sugar in a bowl set over a
pan of hot, but not boiling, water. Whisk by hand or
with an electric mixer until the mixture is thick and
creamy *(page 12)*. Remove the bowl from the pan and
continue to whisk until the whisk, when lifted, leaves a
trail on the mixture's surface. Sift the flour with the
baking powder into another bowl, and mix in 60 g (2
oz) of the pine-nuts. In a third bowl, whisk the egg
whites until stiff, but not dry. Fold the flour mixture, together with one third of the whites, into the whisked
eggs and sugar. Then fold in the remaining whites.

Pour the mixture into the prepared tin and tap the tin
against the work surface to level the sponge. Bake the
batter in the centre of the oven for 10 to 15 minutes,
until well risen, lightly browned and springy when
touched in the centre. Meanwhile, place a piece of
greaseproof paper on the work surface. Mix the
remaining pine-nuts with the caster sugar and sprinkle
them evenly on the paper.

As soon as the cake comes out of the oven, invert it
on to the nuts. Working quickly, detach the lining paper
from the cake and trim away the crisp edges on all four
sides. Spread the apricot purée to the edge of the long
sides and to within 5 mm (½ inch) of the short sides.
With the help of the paper, roll the cake up, starting at
one short side. Grip the roll for 30 seconds, until it
holds its shape. Put the roll on a wire rack to cool.

EDITOR'S NOTE: *Four large oranges will yield about 30 cl (10
fl oz) of orange juice.*

Top: apricot and pine-nut roll; bottom: raspberry roll.

Raspberry Roll

THE CREAM CHEESE FILLING FOR THIS CAKE WOULD MELT IF THE CAKE WERE FILLED AND ROLLED IMMEDIATELY IT CAME OUT OF THE OVEN. SO THAT THE SPONGE SETS IN THE FORM OF A ROLL, IT IS ROLLED ROUND A SHEET OF PAPER WHEN HOT. WHEN THE SPONGE IS COOL BUT STILL FLEXIBLE, IT IS SPREAD WITH THE FILLING AND ROLLED UP AGAIN.

Serves 12
Working time: about 40 minutes
Total time: about 1 hour and 15 minutes

Calories **110**
Protein **5g**
Cholesterol **55mg**
Total fat **4g**
Saturated fat **2g**
Sodium **50mg**

2	eggs	2
60 g	light brown sugar	2 oz
90 g	brown flour	3 oz
½ tsp	baking powder	½ tsp
30 g	fine oatmeal	1 oz
2	egg whites	2
½ tbsp	caster sugar	½ tbsp
175 g	cream cheese	6 oz
2 tbsp	plain low-fat yogurt	2 tbsp
2 tsp	clear honey	2 tsp
125 g	fresh raspberries, or frozen raspberries, thawed	4 oz
60 g	icing sugar	2 oz

Preheat the oven to 180°C (350°F or Mark 4). Grease a 32 by 22 cm (13 by 9 inch) Swiss roll tin. Line it with greaseproof paper and grease the paper.

Put the eggs and brown sugar in a bowl set over a pan of hot, but not boiling, water. Whisk by hand or with an electric mixer until the mixture is thick and creamy (page 12). Remove the bowl from the saucepan and continue to whisk until the whisk, when lifted, leaves a trail on the surface of the mixture. Sift the flour with the baking powder into another bowl, and mix in the oatmeal. In a third bowl, whisk the egg whites until they are stiff but not dry. Fold the flour and oatmeal mixture, together with one third of the egg whites, into the whisked eggs and sugar. Then fold in the remaining egg whites.

Pour the mixture into the prepared tin and tap the tin against the work surface to level the batter. Bake the sponge in the centre of the oven for 10 to 15 minutes until well risen, lightly browned and springy when touched in the centre.

Place a piece of greaseproof paper on the work surface and sprinkle it with the caster sugar. Invert the sponge on to the sugar. Working quickly, detach the lining paper from the sponge. Trim away the crisp edges on all four sides of the sponge. Cover the sponge with a clean sheet of greaseproof paper and roll up the cake with the paper inside (Step 2, below). Transfer the roll to a wire rack to cool.

In a bowl, mix the cream cheese with the yogurt and honey. Reserve 4 raspberries and gently fold the rest of the raspberries into the cream cheese mixture. As soon as the sponge is cool, unroll it and remove the paper. Spread the raspberry filling evenly over the cake to within 5 mm (½ inch) of the short sides and right to the edge of the long sides. Roll up the cake tightly and place it on a serving plate.

Sift the icing sugar into a bowl and mix in 1 tablespoon of boiling water. Press one of the reserved raspberries through a nylon sieve set over the bowl, and stir the juice into the icing to colour it pale pink. Beat the icing until it is smooth and glossy. Dribble the icing over the roll. Halve the remaining raspberries and distribute them over the cake. Serve the raspberry roll when the icing has set.

Rolling a Rectangle of Sponge

1 TRIMMING AND NICKING. After turning the sponge out on to sugar-dredged greaseproof paper, trim away the crisp edges of the sponge with a large knife; if left on, the edges might buckle when the sponge was rolled. To initiate the rolling with ease, cut a shallow groove about 2.5 cm (1 inch) from one short end of the sponge.

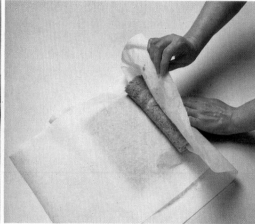

2 ROLLING THE CAKE. Working quickly, cover the sponge with a second piece of greaseproof paper. Lift one end of the bottom sheet of paper so that the sponge starts to roll up with the top sheet of paper inside. Handling the cake through the bottom sheet of paper, nudge the sponge along to complete the roll.

Angel Cake Casket with Mango Filling

Serves 8
Working time: about 30 minutes
Total time: about 5 hours

Calories **150**	5	egg whites	5
Protein **3g**	⅛ tsp	salt	⅛ tsp
Cholesterol **0mg**	175 g	caster sugar	6 oz
Total fat **1g**	½	lemon, finely grated rind only	½
Saturated fat **0g**	1 tbsp	fresh lemon juice	1 tbsp
Sodium **40mg**	30 g	plain flour	1 oz
	30 g	cornflour	1 oz
		icing sugar to decorate	
	Mango filling		
	1	mango	1
	90 g	fromage frais	3 oz
	1½ tsp	gelatine	1½ tsp

Preheat the oven to 180°C (350°F or Mark 4). Lightly grease a 22 by 12 cm (9 by 5 inch) loaf tin. Line its base with greaseproof paper and grease the paper.

Whisk the egg whites with the salt until the whites stand in stiff peaks *(page 12)*. Whisk in 125 g (4 oz) of the caster sugar, 1 tablespoon at a time, until the mix-ture is thick and glossy, then whisk in the lemon rind and juice. Mix the remaining caster sugar with the flours and whisk this in, 1 tablespoon at a time.

Transfer the mixture to the prepared tin and bake it for 35 to 40 minutes until the cake is risen and firm to the touch. Leave it to cool in the tin.

Meanwhile, make the filling. Peel the mango and cut all the flesh away from the stone. Purée the fruit in a food processor or blender: there should be about 20 cl (7 fl oz). Mix the purée with the *fromage frais*. Sprinkle the gelatine on to 2 tablespoons of hot water in a small bowl and stand the bowl in a pan of simmering water for about 10 minutes. When the gelatine has absorbed the water, add a little of the fruit mixture to it. Stir the gelatine-fruit mixture into the bulk of the purée.

Cut down into the cake 2 cm (¾ inch) from the sides to within 2 cm (¾ inch) of the base. Scoop out the centre of the cake with a spoon, to leave a casket with walls and base about 2 cm (¾ inch) thick. Pour the mango purée into the casket. Cover the purée with some of the angel cake trimmings to give the cake its original depth. Cover the cake with plastic film and chill it for at least 2 hours to allow the purée to set.

Using a palette knife, loosen the edges of the cake and invert it on to a platter. Dust with the icing sugar.

EDITOR'S NOTE: *The mango purée may be replaced with a purée of fresh apricots, peaches or gooseberries.*

Vanilla Angel Cake

ANGEL FOOD CAKE CONTAINS NO FAT AT ALL, AND IS SWEET AND
TOOTHSOME ENOUGH TO BE ENJOYED WITHOUT ICING OR GARNISH.
LEAVENED WITH MANY EGG WHITES, THE CAKE DOUBLES IN
SIZE DURING BAKING; FOR SUCCESS WITH A LARGE ANGEL FOOD
CAKE SUCH AS THIS A TUBE CAKE TIN IS ESSENTIAL, SINCE
WITHOUT THE TUBE THE OUTSIDE OF THE VOLUMINOUS CAKE
WOULD DRY OUT BEFORE THE CENTRE HAD SET.

Serves 16
Working time: about 40 minutes
Total time: about 4 hours

Calories **120**
Protein **2g**
Cholesterol **0mg**
Total fat **0g**
Saturated fat **0g**
Sodium **30mg**

150 g	plain flour	5 oz
150 g	icing sugar	5 oz
10	large egg whites	10
1 tsp	cream of tartar	1 tsp
½ tsp	pure vanilla extract	½ tsp
½ tsp	almond extract	½ tsp
175 g	caster sugar	6 oz

Preheat the oven to 190°C (375°F or Mark 5).

Sift the flour and icing sugar together into a bowl.
Put the egg whites, the cream of tartar, vanilla extract
and almond extract in a large, grease-free bowl —
preferably of copper, which reacts chemically with the
egg whites to strengthen the walls of the air bubbles.
Using a hand-held electric whisk or, for the copper
bowl, a large balloon whisk, whisk the egg whites until
they form soft peaks. Whisk in the caster sugar 1
tablespoon at a time, and continue whisking until the
whites form stiff peaks. Fold in the flour and icing
sugar mixture one quarter at a time. Be careful not to
over-stir the mixture: fold only until the flour dis-
appears into the egg white.

Spoon the batter into an ungreased 25 cm (10 inch)
angel cake tin. Run a knife through the batter to expel
excessively large air bubbles. Bake the angel cake in
the centre of the oven for 40 to 45 minutes, until the
mixture springs back when lightly pressed with a
fingertip. Invert the tin on to a wire rack and leave the
cake to stand upside down in its tin for about 2 hours,
until it has cooled completely.

Ease the cake from the side of the tin with a palette
knife; it will then come out easily. Stand the angel food
cake on a serving plate and remove any loose fragments of the browned sponge from the surface of the
cake before serving.

Cherry and Almond Sponge

Serves 16
Working time: about 25 minutes
Total time: about 26 hours

Calories **220**
Protein **3g**
Cholesterol **30g**
Total fat **14g**
Saturated fat **3g**
Sodium **115mg**

175 g	polyunsaturated margarine	6 oz
175 g	caster sugar	6 oz
200 g	plain flour	7 oz
1¼ tsp	baking powder	1¼ tsp
30 g	cornflour	1 oz
30 g	ground almonds	1 oz
2	eggs	2
1 tbsp	lemon juice	1 tbsp
45 g	flaked almonds	1½ oz
90 g	glacé cherries, sliced	3 oz

Preheat the oven to 170°C (325°F or Mark 3). Line an 18 cm (7 inch) square cake tin with non-stick parchment paper.

With a wooden spoon, cream the margarine and sugar together until very pale and fluffy. Sift the flour, baking powder and cornflour together into another bowl, then mix in the ground almonds. Beat the eggs into the creamed mixture, one at a time, following each with 1 tablespoon of the dry ingredients. Add the lemon juice and the remaining dry ingredients. Chop 30 g (1 oz) of the flaked almonds and stir them into the mixture, together with 60 g (2 oz) of the sliced cherries.

Turn the mixture into the prepared tin and level the top. Sprinkle the remaining flaked almonds and sliced cherries over the surface of the cake and cook it for 1¼ to 1½ hours, until firm to the touch and a light golden-brown. Test the cake with a skewer; if the skewer comes out clean, the cake is done. Leave the cake in the tin for a minute or two; it will shrink away from the sides. Turn the cake out on to a wire rack to cool. With the lining paper still in place, wrap the cake in foil and leave it for 24 hours before cutting it.

Spiced Sherry Cake

Serves 16
Working time: about 40 minutes
Total time: about 2 hours

Calories **180**
Protein **3g**
Cholesterol **15mg**
Total fat **8g**
Saturated fat **2g**
Sodium **115mg**

175 g	sultanas	6 oz
4 tbsp	sherry	4 tbsp
125 g	polyunsaturated margarine	4 oz
125 g	light brown sugar	4 oz
1	egg, beaten	1
175 g	plain flour	6 oz
1 tsp	bicarbonate of soda	1 tsp
½ tsp	ground cinnamon	½ tsp
½ tsp	grated nutmeg	½ tsp
⅛ tsp	ground cloves	⅛ tsp
45 g	shelled walnuts, finely chopped	1½ oz
125 g	quark	4 oz
2 tbsp	icing sugar	2 tbsp
16	walnut halves	16

Preheat the oven to 180°C (350°F or Mark 4). Thoroughly grease two 20 cm (8 inch) round sandwich tins. Line their bases with greaseproof paper and grease the paper.

Put the sultanas in a saucepan with the sherry and 4 tablespoons of water and bring the liquid to the boil. Simmer the sultanas gently for about 5 minutes, until the liquid has been absorbed. Remove the pan from the heat and leave the sultanas to become cold, when they will release some of the liquid.

In a mixing bowl, cream the margarine and sugar until pale and fluffy, then beat in the egg with a wooden spoon. Sift the flour, together with the bicarbonate of soda, cinnamon, nutmeg and cloves, into another bowl. Gradually fold the spiced flour, alternately with the sultanas and their liquor, into the creamed margarine. Then fold in the chopped walnuts.

Divide the mixture between the prepared tins and level the surfaces. Cook the sponges for 30 to 35 minutes until firm to the touch. Leave them in the tins for 5 minutes, then loosen the edges of the sponges with a palette knife and turn them out on to a wire rack. Take care not to damage the sponges; the high proportion of liquid makes them very fragile. Leave the sponges to cool with the lining paper still attached.

Carefully peel off the paper and stand one sponge on a serving plate. Spread it with the quark and cover it with the second sponge layer. Dredge the top with the icing sugar and, with a sharp knife, mark the cake into 16 slices. Arrange the walnut halves in a circle round the top of the cake.

Top: spiced sherry cake; bottom: cherry and almond sponge.

Saffron Fruit Cake

MORE COMMONLY KNOWN AS A SPICE FOR SAVOURY DISHES,
SAFFRON IS ALSO INCLUDED FOR ITS GOLDEN COLOUR AND
DISTINCTIVE AROMA IN MANY TRADITIONAL CAKES.

Serves 24
Working time: about 25 minutes
Total time: about 4 hours and 30 minutes

Calories **192**
Protein **3g**
Cholesterol **25mg**
Total fat **8g**
Saturated fat **1g**
Sodium **75mg**

2 tsp	saffron threads	2 tsp
500 g	brown flour	1 lb
4 tsp	baking powder	4 tsp
175 g	polyunsaturated margarine	6 oz
125 g	demerara sugar	4 oz
150 g	dried apricots, four reserved, the rest chopped	5 oz
7	dried figs, three reserved, the rest chopped	7
2	eggs	2
60 g	icing sugar, sieved	2 oz

Preheat the oven to 170°C (325°F or Mark 3). Grease a 20 cm (8 inch) square cake tin. Line it with greaseproof paper and grease the paper. Put the saffron threads in a small saucepan with 17.5 cl (6 fl oz) of water and bring the water to the boil. Remove the pan from the heat and leave the saffron liquid to cool.

Sift the flour and baking powder together into a mixing bowl, and rub in the margarine until the mixture resembles breadcrumbs. Stir in the demerara sugar, chopped apricots, chopped figs, eggs, and 15 cl (5 fl oz) of the saffron liquid. Beat the mixture with a wooden spoon for about 1 minute.

Spoon the mixture into the prepared tin and level the top with a small palette knife. Bake the cake in the centre of the oven until risen, golden-brown and springy in the centre — 55 to 60 minutes. Leave the cake in the tin to cool for 5 minutes, then turn it out and remove the lining paper. Invert the cake on to a wire rack and leave it until completely cold.

Halve the reserved apricots and slice the reserved figs. Arrange the fruit in a line across the top of the cake. Mix the icing sugar thoroughly with the remaining saffron liquid. Dribble the icing over the cake and fruit. Leave it to set.

EDITOR'S NOTE: *The apricots and figs can be replaced by other dried fruits such as prunes, pears and peaches.*

Saffron Bun

Serves 20
Working time: about 40 minutes
Total time: about 14 hours

Calories **160**
Protein **3g**
Cholesterol **10mg**
Total fat **4g**
Saturated fat **2g**
Sodium **10mg**

¼ tsp	saffron threads	¼ tsp
500 g	strong plain flour	1 lb
⅛ tsp	salt	⅛ tsp
90 g	unsalted butter	3 oz
30 g	light brown sugar	1 oz
1	lemon, grated rind only	1
175 g	currants	6 oz
30 g	mixed candied peel, chopped	1 oz
15 g	fresh yeast, or 7 g (¼ oz) dried yeast plus 1 tsp caster sugar	½ oz
15 cl	skimmed milk, tepid	¼ pint
1 tbsp	clear honey	1 tbsp

Infuse the saffron threads in 15 cl (¼ pint) of boiling water overnight, then strain the liquid and set it aside. Grease a 20 cm (8 inch) round cake tin.

Sift the flour and salt into a bowl and rub in the but-ter until the mixture resembles fine breadcrumbs. Stir in the sugar, lemon rind, currants and mixed peel. Blend the fresh yeast or the dried yeast and sugar with the milk. If you use dried yeast, leave the mixture in a warm place for about 15 minutes until frothy.

Warm the saffron liquid in a small saucepan and mix it, together with the yeast blend, into the dry ingredients. Turn the dough out on to a floured surface and knead it for about 5 minutes. Shape the dough to fit the prepared tin. Put the dough in the tin and cover it with oiled plastic film. Leave it in a warm place for 1 to 1½ hours until it has doubled in size and springs back when lightly pressed with a floured finger. Meanwhile, preheat the oven to 200°C (400°F or Mark 6).

Remove the plastic film and bake the bun for 30 minutes. Reduce the temperature to 180°C (350°F or Mark 4) and bake the bun for 25 to 30 minutes more, until it is well risen, browned and firm to the touch. Turn the bun out on to a wire rack. While the bun is still warm, brush its top all over with a wet pastry brush dipped in the clear honey. Leave the bun to cool.

Poppy Seed Plait

Serves 12
Working time: about 1 hour
Total time: about 4 hours

Calories **240**
Protein **6g**
Cholesterol **30mg**
Total fat **10g**
Saturated fat **4g**
Sodium **80mg**

15 g	fresh yeast, or 7 g (¼ oz) dried yeast	½ oz
6 tbsp	milk, tepid	6 tbsp
250 g	strong plain flour	8 oz
⅛ tsp	salt	⅛ tsp
30 g	unsalted butter, melted	1 oz
30 g	caster sugar	1 oz
1	egg, beaten	1
½	lemon, finely grated rind only	½
30 g	icing sugar	1 oz
1 tbsp	fresh lemon juice	1 tbsp

Poppy seed and raisin filling		
90 g	poppy seeds	3 oz
90 g	raisins, chopped	3 oz
¼ litre	milk	8 fl oz
2 tbsp	cornflour	2 tbsp
1	egg yolk	1
30 g	unsalted butter	1 oz
60 g	shelled hazelnuts, toasted and chopped	2 oz

Mix the fresh yeast with the milk and about 1 tablespoon of the flour in a small bowl, or reconstitute the dried yeast according to the manufacturer's instructions, adding 1 tablespoon of the flour. Leave in a warm place until it froths — 10 to 15 minutes.

Sift the remaining flour into a bowl with the salt. Add the butter, sugar, egg, lemon rind and yeast mixture, and work the combination into a soft dough. Knead the dough on a lightly floured surface for 5 minutes. Put the dough in an oiled bowl, cover it with oiled plastic film and leave it in a warm place to rise until doubled in volume — 1 to 2 hours.

Meanwhile, preheat the oven to 200°C (400°F or Mark 6), grease a 22 cm (9 inch) springform tin and make the filling. Put the poppy seeds and raisins in a saucepan with half the milk and simmer gently for 5 to 7 minutes until the poppy seeds have swelled and most of the milk has been absorbed. Mix the cornflour and yolk with the remaining milk and add the mixture to the pan. Cook, stirring, until the mixture thickens. Remove the pan from the heat and stir in the butter. Leave the filling to get cold, then stir in the hazelnuts.

To construct the plait, roll out the dough on a lightly floured surface to a rectangle about 38 by 45 cm (15 by 18 inches). Spread the dough with the poppy seed filling. Roll it into a cylinder, cut it in half lengthwise and twist the two halves together *(below)*.

Place the dough in the prepared tin and join the ends of the braid to make a circle. Bake the poppy seed plait for about 35 minutes, until golden-brown. Transfer it to a wire rack. Combine the icing sugar and lemon juice and brush them over the cake. Leave the cake to cool a little; it is best served just warm.

EDITOR'S NOTE: *To toast hazelnuts, place them on a baking sheet in a 180°C (350°F or Mark 4) oven for 10 minutes.*

Plaiting the Dough

1 ROLLING AND SLICING *Spread the poppy seed filling evenly over the rolled-out dough, leaving about 2.5 cm (1 inch) of dough uncovered round the edge. Roll up the dough from one side to enclose the filling.*

2 DIVIDING THE ROLL. *With a sharp knife, trim the ends of the dough to make a neat cylinder, then cut down the middle of the roll to halve it lengthwise.*

3 TWISTING THE DOUGH *With the cut sides uppermost, lay the middle of one length of poppy seed dough across the middle of the other. Twist the two lengths over each other, working outwards from the centre in one direction, then in the other.*

4 LAYING THE CAKE IN THE TIN. *Keeping the dough cut side up, lift it carefully into the prepared tin. Press the ends together to make a circle.*

Caraway Seed Sponge

Serves 12
Working time: about 25 minutes
Total time: about 3 hours and 30 minutes

Calories **125**
Protein **3g**
Cholesterol **60mg**
Total fat **3g**
Saturated fat **0g**
Sodium **70mg**

3	eggs, separated	3
150 g	light brown sugar	5 oz
125 g	plain flour	4 oz
1 tsp	baking powder	1 tsp
1½ tbsp	cornflour	1½ tbsp
2 tsp	polyunsaturated margarine	2 tsp
1 tbsp	orange flower water	1 tbsp
1 tsp	caraway seeds	1 tsp
	icing sugar to decorate	

Preheat the oven to 200°C (400°F or Mark 6). Grease a 20 cm (8 inch) round cake tin or a petal cake tin approximately 18 cm (7 inches) in diameter. Line the tin with non-stick parchment paper.

Whisk the egg whites until they stand in firm peaks *(page 12)*. Gradually whisk in the brown sugar, 1 tablespoon at a time, then quickly fold in the egg yolks. Sift the flour, baking powder and cornflour together two or three times into another bowl, to aerate them very thoroughly. Heat the margarine in a small saucepan until the margarine melts, then remove the pan from the heat and add the orange flower water and 2 tablespoons of water. Using a metal spoon or a rubber spatula, fold the flour mixture quickly and evenly into the cake mixture, followed by the melted mixture and the caraway seeds. Pour the batter into the prepared tin and bake, until well risen, golden-brown and firm to the touch — 25 to 30 minutes in the round tin, or 30 to 40 minutes in the petal tin.

Turn the cake out on to a wire rack and leave it to cool, then remove the paper. Before serving the cake, sift icing sugar lightly over the top.

Ginger Kugelhopf

A SPECIALITY OF GERMANY, AUSTRIA AND ALSACE, THE KUGELHOPF
IS A YEAST CAKE BAKED IN A TALL, FLUTED RING MOULD.

Serves 12
Working time: about 40 minutes
Total time: about 4 hours

Calories **167**
Protein **4g**
Cholesterol **80mg**
Total fat **7g**
Saturated fat **3g**
Sodium **115mg**

15 g	fresh yeast, or 7 g (¼ oz) dried yeast	½ oz
30 g	caster sugar	1 oz
250 g	strong plain flour	8 oz
½ tsp	salt	½ tsp
1 tsp	ground cinnamon	1 tsp
½ tsp	ground ginger	½ tsp
60 g	unsalted butter, melted	2 oz
3	eggs, beaten	3
30 g	stem ginger, finely chopped	1 oz
30 g	dried apricots, finely chopped	1 oz
30 g	plain chocolate	1 oz
2 tsp	pine-nuts	2 tsp

Mix the yeast and sugar with 4 tablespoons of tepid
water and 1 tablespoon of the flour. Leave the blend in
a warm place for 10 to 15 minutes until it is frothy.

Mix the remaining flour, the salt and the spices in a
bowl. Add the melted butter, beaten eggs, chopped
stem ginger, apricots and yeast blend, and beat the
batter with a wooden spoon until the ingredients have
combined evenly. Cover the batter with oiled plastic
film and leave it in a warm place for 1 to 2 hours, until
it has doubled in volume.

Generously butter a 20 cm (8 inch) kugelhopf mould.
Stir the risen batter quickly, then spoon it into the
prepared mould. Cover it with oiled plastic film and
leave it to rise again until it almost reaches the top of
the mould — 45 minutes to 1 hour. Meanwhile,
preheat the oven to 200°C (400°F or Mark 6).

Remove the plastic film and bake the kugelhopf for
about 30 minutes, until golden-brown and firm to the
touch. Leave it in the mould for 30 minutes, then turn it
out on to a wire rack. When the cake is almost cold,
melt the chocolate in a bowl over a saucepan of hot,
but not boiling, water and dribble it on to the cake from
a spoon or a greaseproof paper piping bag *(page 17)*.
Sprinkle the cake with pine-nuts. Serve it when the
chocolate has set.

Steamed Malt Loaf

COOKED BY STEAMING INSTEAD OF BAKING, THIS LOAF ACQUIRES A
MOIST, RESILIENT TEXTURE. IT IS BEST EATEN TWO OR THREE DAYS
AFTER COOKING, WHEN ITS FLAVOUR HAS FULLY DEVELOPED.

Serves 12
Working time: about 15 minutes
Total time: about 4 hours

Calories **205**
Protein **4g**
Cholesterol **0mg**
Total fat **1g**
Saturated fat **0g**
Sodium **60mg**

200 g	malt extract	7 oz
150 g	wholemeal flour	5 oz
150 g	rye flour	5 oz
150 g	cornmeal	5 oz
1½ tsp	baking powder	1½ tsp
45 cl	buttermilk	¾ pint
150 g	raisins	5 oz
90 g	molasses or black treacle	3 oz

Grease and flour a 25 by 10 cm (10 by 4 inch) loaf tin.

To make the cake, reserve 2 tablespoons of the malt extract for glazing, and stir the remaining malt extract well with all the other ingredients. Pour the batter into the prepared tin and level the surface. Cover the tin loosely with greased foil and set it on a trivet in a fish kettle or large fireproof casserole. Pour boiling water into the fish kettle to come half way up the sides of the loaf tin. Put a lid on the kettle, set it on the stove and adjust the heat so that the water simmers. Cook the loaf for about 2 hours, until it is risen and firm to the touch. Leave it in the tin for 10 minutes.

Turn the malt loaf on to a wire rack. Brush the loaf with the remaining malt extract while still warm, then leave the loaf to cool.

Vinegar Cake

THE VINEGAR REACTS WITH THE BICARBONATE OF SODA TO RELEASE CARBON DIOXIDE, WHICH LEAVENS THE CAKE. THIS DOES NOT AFFECT THE FLAVOUR.

Serves 20
Working time: about 20 minutes
Total time: about 3 hours and 30 minutes

Calories **220**
Protein **2g**
Cholesterol **0mg**
Total fat **8g**
Saturated fat **2g**
Sodium **130mg**

350 g	plain flour	12 oz
125 g	ground rice	4 oz
½ tsp	allspice	½ tsp
175 g	polyunsaturated margarine	6 oz
125 g	raisins	4 oz
125 g	sultanas	4 oz
125 g	mixed candied peel	4 oz
17.5 cl	milk	6 fl oz
3 tbsp	cider vinegar	3 tbsp
1 tsp	bicarbonate of soda	1 tsp
90 g	icing sugar	3 oz
1½ tbsp	fresh lemon juice	1½ tsp

Preheat the oven to 170°C (325°F or Mark 3). Grease a deep 25 by 11 cm (10 by 4½ inch) oblong tin. Line it with greaseproof paper and grease the paper.

Put the flour, ground rice and allspice into a mixing bowl. Add the margarine and rub it in finely with your fingertips until the mixture resembles breadcrumbs. Stir in the raisins, sultanas and candied peel.

Heat the milk in a saucepan until it is tepid. Stir in the vinegar and bicarbonate of soda, which will froth up. Immediately add the frothy liquid to the fruit mixture in the bowl, so as not to lose too much of the gas. Stir with a wooden spoon to blend the ingredients, then beat them to achieve a smooth, soft consistency. Spoon the mixture into the prepared tin. Level the top with a small palette knife.

Bake the cake in the centre of the oven until well risen, golden-brown and springy when touched in the centre — about 1 hour and 10 minutes. Loosen the edges with a small palette knife, turn the cake out of the tin on to a wire rack and remove the lining paper. Leave the cake until it has cooled completely.

With a wooden spoon, beat the icing sugar with the lemon juice in a small bowl until smooth. Spoon the icing into a greaseproof paper piping bag (page 17) and pipe a lattice design over the top of the cake. Leave the cake until the icing has set.

Apricot and Orange Loaf

THE SOYA FLOUR USED IN THIS RECIPE IS HIGH IN PROTEIN: ONE SLICE OF THE CAKE PROVIDES 10 PER CENT OF AN ADULT'S DAILY PROTEIN REQUIREMENT.

Serves 16
Working time: about 30 minutes
Total time: about 4 hours and 30 minutes

Calories **175**
Protein **7g**
Cholesterol **40mg**
Total fat **7g**
Saturated fat **3g**
Sodium **65mg**

125 g	dried apricots, chopped	4 oz
175 g	sultanas	6 oz
15 cl	fresh orange juice	¼ pint
1 tsp	finely grated orange rind	1 tsp
60 g	unsalted butter	2 oz
175 g	soya flour	6 oz
2 tsp	baking powder	2 tsp
60 g	shelled walnuts, chopped	2 oz
60 g	light brown sugar	2 oz
2	eggs, beaten	2
Apricot-walnut topping		
1 tbsp	clear honey	1 tbsp
2 tbsp	fresh orange juice	2 tbsp
30 g	shelled walnuts, chopped	1 oz
6	dried apricots, chopped	6

Preheat the oven to 170°C (325°F or Mark 3). Grease a 22 by 11 cm (9 by 4½ inch) loaf tin. Line the base and the two long sides of the tin with greaseproof paper and grease the paper. Put the apricots, sultanas, orange juice, orange rind and butter in a saucepan. Heat gently, stirring occasionally, until the butter has melted; remove the saucepan from the heat.

Sift the soya flour and baking powder into a bowl. Mix in the walnuts and sugar. With a wooden spoon, stir in the eggs and the butter-fruit mixture from the saucepan, then beat until smooth and glossy.

Spoon the mixture into the prepared tin and level the top with a small palette knife. Bake the loaf in the centre of the oven until risen, lightly browned and springy when touched in the centre — about 1¼ hours. Loosen the edges with a small palette knife, turn the loaf out on to a wire rack and remove the lining paper. Leave the loaf until it is completely cold.

To make the topping, warm the honey and orange juice in a small saucepan. Boil them for 30 seconds, stirring occasionally. Put the walnuts in a small bowl and stir in half of the honey liquid. Add the apricots to the liquid remaining in the pan and heat gently for 1 minute. Arrange the walnuts in a band down the centre of the cake and spread the apricots on either side. Leave for a few minutes to let the topping cool and set.

Left: apricot and orange loaf; right: tea bread with malted grains.

Tea Bread
with Malted Grains

THE MALTED FLOUR USED IN THIS CAKE CONTAINS WHOLE WHEAT
GRAINS, WHICH REMAIN CRUNCHY WHEN COOKED.

Serves 20
Working time: about 20 minutes
Total time: about 4 hours and 30 minutes

Calories **180**
Protein **4g**
Cholesterol **20mg**
Total fat **0g**
Saturated fat **0g**
Sodium **90mg**

175 g	currants	6 oz
175 g	sultanas	6 oz
175 g	raisins	6 oz
125 g	light brown sugar	4 oz
30 cl	warm tea, strained	½ pint
3 tbsp	low-sugar thick-cut marmalade	3 tbsp
500 g	malted wheat flour	1 lb
4 tsp	baking powder	4 tsp
1	egg	1

Preheat the oven to 170°C (325°F or Mark 3). Grease two 20 by 10 cm (8 by 4 inch) loaf tins. Line the base and long sides of each tin with greaseproof paper and grease the paper.

Put the currants, sultanas, raisins and sugar in a mixing bowl with the tea and 2 tablespoons of the marmalade. Stir well, cover the bowl with plastic film and leave the fruit for about 30 minutes to plump up.

When the tea has cooled, sift the flour and baking powder into the fruit mixture, adding the bran and grains left in the sieve. Add the egg and mix the batter well with a wooden spoon.

Divide the mixture equally between the two prepared tins; level the tops with a small palette knife. Bake the loaves in the centre of the oven until risen, lightly browned and springy when touched in the centre — about 1¼ hours. Loosen the edges with a small palette knife, turn the loaves out of the tins on to a wire rack and remove the lining paper. Leave the loaves until they are completely cool.

Heat the remaining marmalade in a small saucepan with 1 teaspoon of water. Boil the marmalade for 30 seconds. Brush the tops of both loaves with marmalade. Leave the loaves to stand until the marmalade has set before slicing and serving them.

EDITOR'S NOTE: *Wrapped separately in plastic film or foil, the loaves will keep well for two weeks in a cool place.*

Spiced Apricot Balmoral Cake

THIS CAKE IS NAMED AFTER THE RIDGED BALMORAL LOAF TIN
IN WHICH IT IS COOKED.

Serves 10
Working time: about 35 minutes
Total time: about 4 hours

Calories **225**
Protein **4g**
Cholesterol **45mg**
Total fat **7g**
Saturated fat **4g**
Sodium **80mg**

200 g	plain flour	7 oz
1½ tsp	baking powder	1½ tsp
½ tsp	grated nutmeg	½ tsp
60 g	polyunsaturated margarine	2 oz
90 g	light brown sugar	3 oz
1	orange, grated rind only	1
90 g	dried apricots, finely chopped	3 oz
1	egg	1
1 tbsp	black treacle	1 tbsp
4½ tbsp	skimmed milk	4½ tbsp
Nutmeg buttercream		
30 g	unsalted butter	1 oz
60 g	icing sugar	2 oz
⅛ tsp	grated nutmeg	⅛ tsp
	fresh orange juice	
7	dried apricots, halved	7

Preheat the oven to 180°C (350°F or Mark 4). Thoroughly grease a 25 cm (10 inch) Balmoral loaf tin or a 22 by 12 cm (9 by 5 inch) loaf tin.

Sift the flour and baking powder into a bowl and mix in the nutmeg. Add the margarine and rub it in until the mixture resembles fine breadcrumbs. Stir in the sugar, orange rind and chopped apricots. In another bowl, whisk together the egg, treacle and skimmed milk; add them to the first bowl and blend the ingredients thoroughly with a wooden spoon.

Turn the mixture into the prepared tin and level the top. Cook the cake for about 50 minutes, until it has risen to the top of the tin; it should be firm to the touch and just beginning to shrink from the sides of the tin. Turn the cake out on to a wire rack and leave it until it has cooled completely.

Meanwhile, make the buttercream. Cream the butter until it is soft, then sift in the icing sugar. Add the nutmeg and beat the mixture with a wooden spoon. Add a few drops of orange juice to give a piping consistency. Spoon the buttercream into a piping bag fitted with a medium-sized star nozzle and pipe a continuous row of shells along the top of the cake. Alternatively, spoon the buttercream down the length of the cake. Decorate the cake with the apricot halves.

Fig Cake Encased in Shortcrust

Serves 10
Working time: about 45 minutes
Total time: about 3 hours and 30 minutes

Calories **230**
Protein **5g**
Cholesterol **50mg**
Total fat **11g**
Saturated fat **5g**
Sodium **120mg**

125 g	dried figs, chopped	4 oz
125 g	dried pears, chopped	4 oz
60 g	dried dates, chopped	2 oz
30 g	unsalted butter, diced	1 oz
2 tbsp	Armagnac	2 tbsp
60 g	shelled walnuts, chopped	2 oz
1	egg, beaten	1
30 g	plain flour	1 oz
½ tsp	ground cinnamon	½ tsp
¼ tsp	ground cloves	¼ tsp
⅛ tsp	salt	⅛ tsp
	icing sugar to decorate	
Pastry crust		
125 g	plain flour	4 oz
60 g	unsalted butter	2 oz
	beaten egg white to glaze	

Put the figs, pears and dates in a saucepan with 6 tablespoons of water. Simmer gently until the fruits are soft and the water has been absorbed — 7 to 8 minutes. Add the butter to the pan and stir the mixture until the butter has melted. Let the fruit-butter mixture cool, then beat in the Armagnac, walnuts, egg, flour, cinnamon, cloves and salt. Set aside.

Preheat the oven to 180°C (350°F or Mark 4).

To make the pastry, sift the flour into a bowl. Rub in the butter and mix in 4 teaspoons of iced water to make a firm dough. Roll out two thirds of the pastry on a lightly floured surface to make a rectangle large enough to cover the base and sides of a 20 by 10 cm (8 by 4 inch) loaf tin. Transfer the pastry to the tin and press it against the base and sides of the tin to cover them with an even thickness.

Spoon the filling into the tin and level the surface. Trim the pastry level with the top of the tin, then fold the pastry walls in over the filling. Add the trimmings to the reserved pastry and roll it out to make a rectangle to fit the top of the cake exactly. Trim the edges of the pastry lid, brush with egg white and lay it, brushed side down, on the filling. Press the edge well so that it sticks to the overlapping pastry walls. Using a fork, mark a criss-cross pattern and decorative border on the pastry lid. Brush the lid with egg white.

Bake the cake for 40 to 45 minutes, until the pastry is pale golden. Let the cake stand in the tin for 10 minutes, then transfer it to a wire rack and leave it to cool. Dust the fig cake with icing sugar before serving.

Tropical Fruit Cake

Serves 24
Working time: about 30 minutes
Total time: about 5 hours

Calories **275**
Protein **4g**
Cholesterol **45mg**
Total fat **10g**
Saturated fat **3g**
Sodium **145mg**

250 g	polyunsaturated margarine	8 oz
250 g	light brown sugar	8 oz
4	eggs	4
350 g	plain flour	12 oz
3 tsp	baking powder	3 tsp
45 g	angelica, chopped	1½ oz
125 g	dried papaya, chopped	4 oz
125 g	dried pineapple, chopped	4 oz
75 g	shredded coconut	2½ oz
60 g	banana chips, crushed	2 oz
2 tbsp	skimmed milk	2 tbsp
1 tbsp	apricot jam without added sugar	1 tbsp

Preheat the oven to 180°C (350°F or Mark 4). Grease a 22 cm (9 inch) round cake tin and line it with non-stick parchment paper.

Put the margarine, sugar and eggs in a mixing bowl. Sift in the flour and baking powder. Reserve 15 g

(1½ oz) of the angelica, 30 g (1 oz) of the dried papaya, 30 g (1 oz) of the dried pineapple and 15 g (½ oz) of the shredded coconut for decoration. Roughly chop the rest of the shredded coconut. Add the remaining angelica, papaya, pineapple and chopped coconut to the bowl, then add the banana chips and the skimmed milk. Mix until the ingredients are thoroughly blended, then beat the batter firmly with a wooden spoon for 2 minutes until it is smooth. Turn it into the prepared tin and level the top.

Cook the fruit cake for about 2 hours, until it is well browned and firm to the touch; a skewer inserted in the centre should come out clean.

Cool the cake for 5 minutes in the tin, then turn it out on to a wire rack and leave it to cool completely. Peel off the lining paper. Warm the jam in a small saucepan and brush it over the top of the cake. Sprinkle the top of the cake with the reserved tropical fruits.

Farmhouse Fruit Cake

THE OVERNIGHT SOAKING OF THE INGREDIENTS IN TEA MAKES
THIS CAKE VERY MOIST.

Serves 10
Working time: about 20 minutes
Total time: about 1½ days

Calories **210**
Protein **2g**
Cholesterol **0mg**
Total fat **7g**
Saturated fat **2g**
Sodium **170mg**

250 g	plain flour	8 oz
½ tsp	allspice	½ tsp
90 g	polyunsaturated margarine	3 oz
90 g	light brown sugar	3 oz
125 g	sultanas	4 oz
60 g	currants	2 oz
½	lemon, grated rind only	½
1 tsp	bicarbonate of soda	1 tsp
2 tbsp	lemon juice	2 tbsp
¼ litre	cold tea	8 fl oz
1 tsp	sugar crystals	1 tsp

Grease a 16 to 18 cm (6½ to 7 inch) round cake tin and line it with non-stick parchment paper.

Sift the flour and allspice together in a bowl. Add the margarine and rub it in until the mixture resembles fine breadcrumbs. Stir in the brown sugar, sultanas, currants and lemon rind until they are evenly distributed. Whisk the bicarbonate of soda into the lemon juice and add this mixture, together with the cold tea, to the dry ingredients. When the ingredients are thoroughly combined, turn the mixture into the prepared tin, level the top and leave the mixture to stand overnight.

The following day, preheat the oven to 170°C (325°F or Mark 3). Sprinkle the cake mixture with the sugar crystals and cook it for about 1½ hours, until a skewer inserted in its centre comes out clean. Turn the cake out on to a wire rack and leave it to cool. With the lining paper still in place, wrap the cake in foil and store it for 24 hours; it crumbles if sliced sooner.

Stollen

STOLLEN, THE GERMAN YEAST-LEAVENED CHRISTMAS CAKE, IS
USUALLY RICH IN BUTTER AND SOMETIMES INCLUDES GROUND
ALMONDS; THIS VERSION, WITH LESS BUTTER AND NO ALMONDS, IS
LIGHTER BUT STILL DELICIOUSLY FLAVOURED WITH DRIED FRUITS
AND RUM. UNLIKE MOST YEAST CAKES, STOLLEN SHOULD BE MADE
WITH PLAIN FLOUR RATHER THAN STRONG FLOUR, TO GIVE A SOFT,
SLIGHTLY CRUMBLY TEXTURE.

Serves 24
Working time: about 40 minutes
Total time: about 7 hours

Calories **135**
Protein **3g**
Cholesterol **20mg**
Total fat **4g**
Saturated fat **2g**
Sodium **15mg**

30 g	fresh yeast or 15 g (½ oz) dried yeast	1 oz
60 g	vanilla-flavoured caster sugar	2 oz
6 tbsp	skimmed milk	6 tbsp
2 tbsp	dark rum	2 tbsp
400 g	plain flour	14 oz
100 g	unsalted butter	3½ oz
1	egg, beaten	1
60 g	raisins	2 oz
60 g	currants	2 oz
60 g	mixed candied peel, chopped	2 oz
30 g	glacé cherries, chopped	1 oz
30 g	angelica, chopped	1 oz
2 tbsp	icing sugar	2 tbsp

In a small bowl, blend the yeast with 2 tablespoons of
warm water. If using dried yeast, add 1 teaspoon of
the sugar to the yeast and water, and leave the yeast
to blend in a warm place for about 20 minutes until it
froths; fresh yeast can be used immediately.

Warm the skimmed milk in a saucepan. Remove the
pan from the heat and dissolve the sugar in the milk;
add the rum and the yeast liquid. Sift the flour into a
large bowl and make a well in the centre. Cut 90 g
(3 oz) of the butter into bean-sized pieces and add
them to the flour. Add the yeast mixture and the
beaten egg, raisins, currants, mixed peel, cherries and
angelica. Mix the ingredients with a palette knife and
knead the dough for 10 minutes by hand on a lightly
floured surface or for 4 to 5 minutes in a large electric
mixer fitted with a dough hook.

Flour the bowl and return the dough to it. Cover the
dough with oiled plastic film and leave it to rise in a
warm place until it has doubled in size — about 2
hours. (It takes a long time because of all the fruit.)
Knock back the dough and knead it for 2 to 3
minutes until smooth. On a lightly floured surface, roll
the dough out into a rectangle approximately 30 by 20
cm (12 by 8 inches). Fold one long side of the rectangle over just beyond the centre, then fold the other
long side to overlap the first. Press down lightly to

secure the flap in position and move the cake on to a well-greased baking sheet. Melt the remaining butter and brush it over the surface of the stollen. Put the cake in a warm place for 20 to 30 minutes, until it has almost doubled in size. Meanwhile, preheat the oven to 190°C (375°F or Mark 5).

Cook the stollen for about 40 minutes, until it is well risen and browned and the loaf sounds hollow when tapped on its base. Transfer the stollen to a wire rack and leave it to cool completely. Dredge the stollen with the icing sugar before serving.

EDITOR'S NOTE: *The stollen will freeze well for up to two months. Do not add the icing sugar until it has thawed.*

Dundee Cake

WITH ITS VERY HIGH PROPORTION OF FRUIT, THIS MOIST, DARK CAKE IS FULL OF FLAVOUR YET LIGHT IN TEXTURE.

Serves 28
Working time: about 20 minutes
Total time: about 7 hours

Calories **215**
Protein **3g**
Cholesterol **40mg**
Total fat **8g**
Saturated fat **2g**
Sodium **95mg**

250 g	currants	8 oz
250 g	sultanas	8 oz
250 g	raisins	8 oz
60 g	mixed candied peel, chopped	2 oz
60 g	glacé cherries, quartered	2 oz
1	orange, grated rind and juice	1
250 g	wholemeal flour	8 oz
1 tsp	baking powder	1 tsp
90 g	medium oatmeal	3 oz
2 tsp	ground mixed spice	2 tsp
125 g	light brown sugar	4 oz
2 tbsp	molasses	2 tbsp
175 g	polyunsaturated margarine	6 oz
4	eggs, beaten	4
60 g	blanched almonds	2 oz

Preheat the oven to 140°C (275°F or Mark 1). Grease a deep, 18 cm (7 inch) square cake tin and double-line it with greaseproof paper. Grease the paper. To prevent the sides and base of the cake from scorching during the long cooking, tie a double thickness of brown paper round the outside of the tin and stand the tin on a baking sheet double-lined with brown paper.

Stir the currants, sultanas, raisins, mixed peel, glacé cherries, orange rind and juice together in a mixing bowl. Sift the flour and baking powder together into another bowl, adding the bran left in the sieve. Mix in the oatmeal, mixed spice, sugar, molasses, margarine and eggs. Beat the mixture with a wooden spoon for 2 to 3 minutes until smooth and glossy.

Stir the fruit into the cake batter. Spoon the batter into the cake tin and level the top with a small palette knife. Arrange the almonds in rows on the cake.

Bake the cake in the centre of the oven until risen and dark brown — 2½ to 3 hours. Test the cake by inserting a warm skewer or cocktail stick into the centre of the cake. If it is clean when removed, the cake is cooked; otherwise, return the cake to the oven and test it at 15-minute intervals.

Leave the cake to cool in the tin, then turn it out and remove the lining paper.

EDITOR'S NOTE: *Because the fruit retains moisture, this cake will keep for up to one month if wrapped in plastic film or foil and stored in a cold, dry place.*

Coffee Walnut Cake

Serves 14
Working time: about 20 minutes
Total time: about 2 hours and 30 minutes

Calories **210**
Protein **4g**
Cholesterol **30mg**
Total fat **13g**
Saturated fat **2g**
Sodium **185mg**

125 g	polyunsaturated margarine	4 oz
60 g	light brown sugar	2 oz
4 tbsp	clear honey	4 tbsp
2	eggs, beaten	2
2 tbsp	strong black coffee, cooled	2 tbsp
250 g	brown flour	8 oz
3 tsp	baking powder	3 tsp
90 g	shelled walnuts, roughly chopped	3 oz
10	shelled walnut halves	10

Preheat the oven to 170°C (325°F or Mark 3). Grease a deep 20 cm (8 inch) round cake tin. Line it with greaseproof paper and grease the paper.

Put the margarine, sugar and honey into a mixing bowl. Beat them together with a wooden spoon until light and fluffy. Add the beaten egg a little at a time, beating well after each addition. Beat in the coffee.

Sift the brown flour and baking powder into the batter. Using a spatula or large metal spoon, fold the flour into the batter, then mix in the chopped walnuts. Spoon the cake mixture into the prepared tin. Level the top with a small palette knife and arrange the walnut halves round the edge.

Bake the cake in the centre of the oven until risen, lightly browned and springy when touched in the centre — 50 to 55 minutes. Loosen the edges of the cake with a small palette knife, turn it out on to a wire rack and remove the greaseproof paper. Leave the cake to cool before serving.

Clove and Apple Loaf

Serves 20
Working time: about 20 minutes
Total time: about 4 hours

Calories **150**
Protein **4g**
Cholesterol **20mg**
Total fat **5g**
Saturated fat **0g**
Sodium **80mg**

2	red dessert apples, cored and chopped	2
60 g	shelled pecan nuts, chopped	2 oz
60 g	shelled hazelnuts, chopped	2 oz
2 tbsp	clear honey	2 tbsp
1 tbsp	safflower oil	1 tbsp
125 g	light brown sugar	4 oz
15 cl	dry cider	¼ pint
1	egg, beaten	1
250 g	wholemeal flour	8 oz
125 g	rye flour	4 oz
4 tsp	baking powder	4 tsp
1 tsp	ground cloves	1 tsp

Preheat the oven to 170°C (325°F or Mark 3). Grease a 30 by 10 cm (12 by 4 inch) loaf tin. Line it with grease-proof paper and grease the paper.

Put the apples, pecan nuts, hazelnuts, honey, oil, sugar, cider and egg in a mixing bowl. Mix them well together using a wooden spoon. Sift in the wholemeal flour with the rye flour, baking powder and cloves, adding the bran left in the sieve. Stir until the batter is well blended, then beat for 1 minute until it is glossy. Spoon the batter into the prepared tin and level the top with a small palette knife.

Bake the loaf in the centre of the oven until risen, lightly browned and springy when touched in the centre — about 1 hour and 20 minutes. Loosen the edges with a small palette knife and turn the loaf out of the tin on to a wire rack. Remove the lining paper and leave the loaf until it has cooled completely.

Raisin and Ginger Buttermilk Cake

BUTTERMILK IS A LOW-FAT DAIRY FOOD, TRADITIONALLY PRODUCED AS A BY-PRODUCT OF BUTTER-MAKING BUT NOWADAYS OFTEN SPECIALLY PREPARED BY THICKENING SKIMMED MILK WITH A BACTERIAL CULTURE. THIS FRUIT CAKE IS LEAVENED BY THE CARBON DIOXIDE GAS PRODUCED WHEN THE BICARBONATE OF SODA ENCOUNTERS THE ACID IN THE BUTTERMILK.

Serves 16
Working time: about 30 minutes
Total time: about 5 hours

Calories **220**
Protein **3g**
Cholesterol **0mg**
Total fat **8g**
Saturated fat **2g**
Sodium **130mg**

175 g	plain flour	6 oz
175 g	wholemeal flour	6 oz
½ tsp	ground cinnamon	½ tsp
¼ tsp	ground ginger	¼ tsp
¼ tsp	ground mixed spice	¼ tsp
150 g	polyunsaturated margarine	5 oz
125 g	light brown sugar	4 oz
1	lemon, grated rind only	1
90 g	currants	3 oz
90 g	raisins	3 oz
60 g	mixed candied peel, chopped	2 oz
¼ litre	buttermilk	8 fl oz
1 tbsp	black treacle	1 tbsp
¾ tsp	bicarbonate of soda	¾ tsp

Preheat the oven to 170°C (325°F or Mark 3). Line a 22 by 12 cm (9 by 5 inch) loaf tin with non-stick parchment paper.

Sift the plain flour into a bowl and mix in the wholemeal flour, cinnamon, ginger and mixed spice. Add the margarine and rub it in until the mixture resembles fine breadcrumbs. Mix in the sugar, lemon rind, currants, raisins and peel. Heat the buttermilk gently in a saucepan, then stir in the treacle until it melts. Add the bicarbonate of soda to the pan and stir until it froths. Combine this liquid with the dry ingredients and mix until they are evenly blended.

Turn the mixture into the prepared tin and level the top. Cook the buttermilk cake for about 1¼ hours, until it is well risen and firm to the touch; a skewer inserted in the centre should come out clean. Turn the buttermilk cake out on to a wire rack and leave it to cool completely before removing the lining paper.

Banana Tofu Cake

TOFU, ALSO KNOWN AS BEAN CURD, IS A PROTEIN-RICH EXTRACT OF
SOYA BEANS. IT HAS A MILD TASTE AND A TEXTURE SIMILAR TO THAT
OF CURD CHEESE. AGAR, A SEAWEED PRODUCT, HAS GELLING
PROPERTIES AND IS USED BY VEGETARIANS IN PLACE OF GELATINE.

Serves 10
Working time: about 30 minutes
Total time: about 3 hours

Calories **290**
Protein **20g**
Cholesterol **20mg**
Total fat **10g**
Saturated fat **4g**
Sodium **35mg**

175 g	stoned fresh dates, chopped	6 oz
30 cl	fresh orange juice	½ pint
175 g	peeled bananas, sliced	6 oz
500 g	tofu	1 lb
1 tbsp	agar flakes	1 tbsp
1 tsp	finely grated lemon rind	1 tsp
½ tsp	ground mixed spice	½ tsp
1 tbsp	apricot jam without added sugar	1 tbsp
1 tbsp	finely chopped skinned toasted hazelnuts	1 tbsp
Spicy oat base		
125 g	wholemeal flour	4 oz
125 g	rolled oats	4 oz
75 g	unsalted butter, melted	2½ oz
30 g	malt extract	1 oz
1 tsp	ground mixed spice	1 tsp

Preheat the oven to 180°C (350°F or Mark 4). To make
the spicy oat base, combine the flour, oats, butter, malt
extract and mixed spice in a bowl. Press them into the
bottom of a 20 cm (8 inch) springform tin. Bake the
base for 15 minutes, then leave it to cool.

Simmer the dates in the orange juice for about 12
minutes, until the dates are very soft. Put the dates
and juice in a food processor or blender together with
the bananas, tofu, agar flakes, lemon rind and mixed
spice. Blend to a purée. Spoon the purée over the oat
base and level the surface. Bake the cake for 40 to 45
minutes, until it is firm when pressed in the centre.
Leave the cake to cool in the tin.

While the cake is cooling, heat the apricot jam in a
small saucepan. Sieve the jam into a bowl and brush it
over the surface of the cake. Sprinkle the chopped
hazelnuts round the edge of the cake.

EDITOR'S NOTE: *Two large peeled bananas weigh about 175 g
(6 oz). Four large oranges yield about 30 cl (½ pint) of juice. To
toast and skin hazelnuts, place them on a baking sheet in a
180°C (350°F or Mark 4) oven for 10 minutes. Enfold the nuts
in a towel and loosen the skins by rubbing briskly.*

Pear and Orange Upside-Down Cake

Serves 10
Working time: about 20 minutes
Total time: about 2 hours and 30 minutes

Calories **160**
Protein **2g**
Cholesterol **0mg**
Total fat **5g**
Saturated fat **0g**
Sodium **110mg**

2	pears, peeled and sliced	2
1 tsp	fresh lemon juice	1 tsp
3	oranges, peel and pith sliced off (page 14)	3
175 g	brown flour	6 oz
3 tsp	baking powder	3 tsp
90 g	light brown sugar	3 oz
3 tbsp	safflower oil	3 tbsp
½ tsp	pure vanilla extract	½ tsp
1 tbsp	clear honey	1 tbsp
2 tbsp	fresh orange juice	2 tbsp

Preheat the oven to 170°C (325°F or Mark 3). Grease a 20 cm (8 inch) round sandwich tin. Line its base with greaseproof paper and grease the paper.

Sprinkle the pear slices with lemon juice. Cut two of the oranges into segments, discarding the membranes (page 14). From the third orange, cut one slice across the grain of the segments. Put this slice in the middle of the prepared tin. Radiating out from the central slice of orange, arrange alternate orange segments and pear slices to cover the base of the tin.

Sift the flour and baking powder into a bowl, then stir in the sugar. Whisk the oil with the vanilla extract and 15 cl (¼ pint) of cold water until well blended. Make a well in the centre of the dry ingredients and stir in the oil mixture. Beat well with a wooden spoon until the batter is smooth and glossy.

Pour the batter over the fruit in the tin and level the top with a small palette knife. Bake in the centre of the oven until well risen, lightly browned and springy when touched in the centre — 40 to 45 minutes.

Leave the cake in the tin for 5 minutes, then loosen its edge with a palette knife. Turn the cake out of the tin on to a wire rack and remove the lining paper. Leave the cake to cool.

Heat the honey and orange juice gently in a small saucepan, stirring to blend the mixture. Boil the liquid for about 30 seconds until it is syrupy. Quickly brush the oranges and pears with the glaze.

Pineapple Cake

THE PINEAPPLE MAKES THIS CAKE VERY MOIST. AS A RESULT, THE
CURRANTS DO NOT REMAIN DISTRIBUTED THROUGHOUT THE BATTER
BUT FORM A LAYER AT THE BOTTOM OF THE CAKE.

Serves 12
Working time: about 25 minutes
Total time: about 3 hours

Calories **220**
Protein **4g**
Cholesterol **40mg**
Total fat **10g**
Saturated fat **2g**
Sodium **95mg**

125 g	polyunsaturated margarine	4 oz
125 g	light brown sugar	4 oz
2	eggs	2
200 g	plain flour	7 oz
1¾ tsp	baking powder	1¾ tsp
125 g	currants	4 oz
200 g	fresh pineapple flesh	7 oz

Preheat the oven to 170°C (325°F or Mark 3). Line a 20
cm (8 inch) round cake tin with greaseproof paper and
grease the paper.

Using a wooden spoon, cream the margarine and
sugar together until light and fluffy. Beat in the eggs

one at a time, following each with 1 tablespoon of the
flour. Sift in the remaining flour, together with the
baking powder. With a metal spoon or rubber spatula,
fold the flour into the batter, then mix in the currants.
Purée the pineapple in a food processor or blender,
and fold it into the cake mixture.

Turn the mixture into the prepared tin and level the
top. Bake the pineapple cake for about 1¼ hours, until
it is firm to the touch and golden-brown. Leave the
cake in the tin for 10 minutes, then turn it on to a wire
rack and leave it to cool. Remove the lining paper.

SUGGESTED ACCOMPANIMENT: *sliced fresh pineapple.*

Plum Pizza

Serves 10
Working time: about 45 minutes
Total time: about 2 hours and 30 minutes

Calories **240**			
Protein **7g**	30 g	skimmed milk powder	1 oz
Cholesterol **105mg**	90 g	medium-fat curd cheese	3 oz
Total fat **8g**	90 g	thick Greek yogurt	3 oz
Saturated fat **3g**	2 tbsp	clear honey	2 tbsp
Sodium **35mg**	1 tsp	ground cinnamon	1 tsp
	750 g	red plums, stoned and quartered	1½ lb
	2 tbsp	apricot jam without added sugar	2 tbsp
	Yeast dough		
	15 g	fresh yeast, or (7 g) ¼ oz dried yeast	½ oz
	6 tbsp	milk, tepid	6 tbsp
	30 g	caster sugar	1 oz
	250 g	strong plain flour	8 oz
	⅛ tsp	salt	⅛ tsp
	30 g	unsalted butter, melted	1 oz
	1	egg, beaten	1

To make the dough, mix the yeast with the milk, the sugar and 1 tablespoon of the flour. Leave the liquid in a warm place for 10 to 15 minutes to froth. Then mix the liquid with the salt, butter, egg and remaining flour, and knead the dough on a lightly floured surface for 5 minutes. Put the dough in an oiled bowl, cover it with oiled plastic film and leave it to rise for about 1 hour, until doubled in volume.

Meanwhile, preheat the oven to 200°C (400°F or Mark 6). Beat the milk powder, curd cheese, yogurt, honey and cinnamon together with a wooden spoon and set aside. Grease a 25 cm (10 inch) sandwich tin.

On a lightly floured surface, roll out the risen dough to approximately the size of the prepared tin. Press the dough against the tin's base and sides. Spread the cheese mixture over the dough and arrange the plums on the top, cut side down. Bake the pizza for about 30 minutes, until the dough is golden-brown and the plums are tender.

Leave the pizza to cool for 15 minutes, then warm the jam in a small saucepan and brush it over the plums. Serve the pizza just warm.

EDITOR'S NOTE: *Instead of plums, the pizza can be made with peaches, apricots or thinly sliced apples or pears.*

Banana Layer Cake

Serves 12
Working time: about 30 minutes
Total time: about 2 hours

Calories **235**
Protein **5g**
Cholesterol **45mg**
Total fat **11g**
Saturated fat **2g**
Sodium **70mg**

90 g	soft brown sugar	3 oz
10 cl	safflower oil	3½ fl oz
2	eggs	2
3	bananas, peeled and mashed	3
1 tsp	finely grated lemon rind	1 tsp
175 g	wholemeal flour	6 oz
1½ tsp	baking powder	1½ tsp
¼ tsp	ground allspice	¼ tsp
60 g	rolled oats	2 oz
½ tsp	icing sugar	½ tsp
Yogurt-banana filling		
175 g	thick Greek yogurt	6 oz
1	banana, peeled and finely chopped	1

Preheat the oven to 180°C (350°F or Mark 4). Grease a 22 by 18 cm (9 by 7 inch) cake tin; line the base with greaseproof paper and grease the paper.

Whisk together the brown sugar, oil and eggs until thick and pale. Stir in the mashed bananas and lemon rind. Sift the flour with the baking powder and allspice into the banana mixture, adding the bran left in the sieve. Add the oats and then fold the ingredients together with a metal spoon. Transfer the batter to the prepared tin and level the surface. Bake the banana cake for about 30 minutes, until risen and firm to the touch. Leave it in the tin for 10 minutes, then transfer it to a wire tray to cool.

Remove the paper and trim the edges. Split the cake in half horizontally and halve each piece again.

To make the filling, mix the yogurt with the chopped banana. Sandwich the four layers of cake together with the banana mixture and dust the top of the cake with the icing sugar.

Apple and Date Cake

Serves 14
Working time: about 20 minutes
Total time: about 4 hours

Calories **240**
Protein **5g**
Cholesterol **50mg**
Total fat **7g**
Saturated fat **1g**
Sodium **100mg**

300 g	wholemeal flour	10 oz
3 tsp	baking powder	3 tsp
2 tsp	ground mixed spice	2 tsp
½ tsp	grated nutmeg	½ tsp
125 g	dark brown sugar	4 oz
250 g	dried dates, chopped	8 oz
500 g	dessert apples, peeled and cored	1 lb
15 cl	medium-sweet cider	¼ pint
3	eggs	3
8 cl	safflower oil	3 fl oz
2 tbsp	clear honey	2 tbsp

Preheat the oven to 180°C (350°F or Mark 4). Grease a deep, 20 cm (8 inch) round cake tin. Line the base with greaseproof paper and grease the paper.

Sift the flour and baking powder into a bowl, adding the bran left in the sieve. Stir in the mixed spice, nutmeg, sugar and dates. Grate half the apples and add them to the dry ingredients with the cider, eggs and oil. With a wooden spoon, beat the ingredients together thoroughly and turn them into the prepared tin.

Slice the remaining apples thinly and overlap the slices in two circles on top of the cake; stand a few slices upright in the centre. Bake for 1¼ to 1½ hours, until a skewer inserted in the centre comes out clean.

Turn the cake on to a wire rack and remove the lining paper. While the cake is still warm, boil the honey for 1 minute in a small saucepan. Brush the apples with the honey, then leave the cake to cool.

Apple Cake with Currants

Serves 16
Working time: about 25 minutes
Total time: about 5 hours

Calories **240**
Protein **3g**
Cholesterol **35mg**
Total fat **7g**
Saturated fat **1g**
Sodium **110mg**

175 g	plain flour	6 oz
½ tsp	bicarbonate of soda	½ tsp
1 tsp	ground mixed spice	1 tsp
½ tsp	ground cinnamon	½ tsp
125 g	wholemeal flour	4 oz
125 g	polyunsaturated margarine	4 oz
125 g	light brown sugar	4 oz
2	eggs	2
1 tbsp	fresh lemon juice	1 tbsp
175 g	currants	6 oz
125 g	sultanas	4 oz
60 g	mixed candied peel, chopped	2 oz
1	lemon, grated rind only	1
250 g	dessert apples, peeled, cored and coarsely grated	8 oz
2 tbsp	caster sugar	2 tbsp

Preheat the oven to 180°C (350°F or Mark 4). Grease a 20 cm (8 inch) round cake tin and line it with non-stick parchment paper.

Sift the plain flour into a bowl, together with the bicarbonate of soda, mixed spice and cinnamon. Mix in the wholemeal flour. In another bowl, cream the margarine and brown sugar until very pale and fluffy. With a wooden spoon, beat in the eggs one at a time, following each with 1 tablespoon of the flour mixture, then add the lemon juice and fold in the remaining flour. Add the currants, sultanas, mixed candied peel, lemon rind and grated apples, and mix all the ingredients together thoroughly.

Spoon the mixture into the prepared tin and level the top. Sprinkle the caster sugar evenly over the surface of the cake. Cook the cake for 1¼ to 1½ hours until golden-brown and firm to the touch. Leave the cake in the tin for 10 minutes, then turn it out on to a wire rack and leave until cool before removing the lining paper.

Harvest Cake

Serves 28
Working time: about 40 minutes
Total time: about 7 hours

Calories **185**
Protein **5g**
Cholesterol **30mg**
Total fat **6g**
Saturated fat **2g**
Sodium **120mg**

250 g	cooking apples, peeled, cored and chopped	8 oz
250 g	pears, peeled, cored and chopped	8 oz
250 g	plums, stoned and chopped	8 oz
175 g	raisins	6 oz
17.5 cl	apple juice or grape juice	6 fl oz
350 g	malted wheat flour	12 oz
175 g	light brown sugar	6 oz
175 g	polyunsaturated margarine	6 oz
2 tsp	ground mixed spice	2 tsp
3	eggs	3
150 g	wholewheat flakes	5 oz
Cheese and fruit topping		
1	green-skinned dessert apple	1
1	pear	1
1 tbsp	lemon juice	1 tbsp
175 g	quark	6 oz
1 tbsp	plain low-fat yogurt	1 tbsp
1 tsp	clear honey	1 tsp

Grease a 25 by 20 cm (10 by 8 inch) oblong tin. Line it with greaseproof paper and grease the paper. Mix the chopped apples, pears and plums with the raisins and apple juice or grape juice in a bowl. Cover the bowl and leave for up to 1 hour, to plump the fruit. Meanwhile, preheat the oven to 170°C (325°F or Mark 3).

Put the flour, sugar, margarine, mixed spice and eggs in a mixing bowl. Stir them together with a wooden spoon and beat the mixture until it is smooth and glossy. Add the soaked fruit and the wheat flakes to the cake mixture a little at a time, stirring well after each addition. Spoon the mixture into the prepared tin and level the top with a small palette knife. Bake the cake in the centre of the oven until risen, lightly browned and springy when touched in the centre — 1½ hours to 1¾ hours.

Loosen the edges of the cake with a small palette knife, turn it out of the tin on to a wire rack and remove the lining paper. Leave the cake to cool completely.

To make the cheese and fruit topping, core and thinly slice the apple and pear. Sprinkle the slices with lemon juice to stop discoloration. Put the quark in a bowl with the yogurt and honey and blend them together. Spread the cheese mixture over the top of the cake and arrange alternate pairs of apple and pear slices down the centre.

Courgette Cake

THE COURGETTES IN THIS CAKE SUPPLY MOISTURE AND A FLAVOUR
THAT MARRIES REMARKABLY WELL WITH THE SWEET INGREDIENTS.

Serves 12
Working time: about 15 minutes
Total time: about 2 hours and 30 minutes

Calories **225**
Protein **4g**
Cholesterol **25mg**
Total fat **9g**
Saturated fat **3g**
Sodium **155mg**

250 g	courgettes, coarsely grated	8 oz
125 g	fresh dates, stoned and chopped	4 oz
60 g	raisins	2 oz
4 tbsp	clear honey	4 tbsp
125 g	polyunsaturated margarine	4 oz
125 g	light brown sugar	4 oz
1	egg, beaten	1
250 g	brown flour	8 oz
2 tsp	baking powder	2 tsp

Preheat the oven to 170°C (325°F or Mark 3). Grease a shallow 22 cm (9 inch) cake tin. Line its base with greaseproof paper and grease the paper.

Stir the courgettes with the dates, raisins and honey in a mixing bowl. In another bowl, cream the margarine and sugar together until light and fluffy. Add the eggs with 2 tablespoons of water, and beat with a wooden spoon until the mixture is smooth and glossy.

Sift the flour with the baking powder, and fold them into the creamed margarine mixture using a spatula or large spoon. Then fold in the courgettes, dates and raisins. Spoon the mixture into the prepared tin and level the top with a small palette knife. Bake the courgette cake in the centre of the oven until risen, lightly browned and springy when touched in the centre — 55 to 60 minutes.

Loosen the cake from the sides of the tin with a small palette knife. Turn the cake on to a wire rack and remove the lining paper. Leave the cake until it has cooled completely before serving.

Pumpkin Cake

Serves 16
Working time: about 20 minutes
Total time: about 3 hours

Calories **170**
Protein **4g**
Cholesterol **15mg**
Total fat **9g**
Saturated fat **3g**
Sodium **180mg**

500 g	pumpkin, peeled and chopped	1 lb
175 g	brown flour	6 oz
3 tsp	baking powder	3 tsp
1 tsp	ground cinnamon	1 tsp
125 g	medium oatmeal	4 oz
60 g	light brown sugar	2 oz
90 g	polyunsaturated margarine	3 oz
1	egg, beaten	1
Honey-cheese topping		
250 g	medium-fat curd cheese	8 oz
2 tbsp	plain low-fat yogurt	2 tbsp
4 tsp	clear honey	4 tsp
2 tbsp	pumpkin seeds, lightly browned	2 tbsp

Preheat the oven to 170°C (325°F or Mark 3). Grease an 18 cm (7 inch) square cake tin. Line the tin with greaseproof paper and grease the paper.

Put the pumpkin in a saucepan with 4 tablespoons of water. Bring the water to the boil and simmer for 2 to 3 minutes, or until the pumpkin is tender. Strain the pumpkin and purée it in a blender or food processor. You should have at least ¼ litre (8 fl oz) of purée. Leave it to cool.

Sift the flour into a bowl with the baking powder and cinnamon. Add the oatmeal and brown sugar, and stir. Rub in the margarine with the fingertips until the mixture resembles breadcrumbs.

Stir in the egg and ¼ litre (8 fl oz) of the pumpkin purée, then beat the mixture with a wooden spoon for 1 minute until smooth. Spoon the mixture into the tin and level the top with a small palette knife.

Bake the cake in the centre of the oven until risen, golden-brown and springy when touched in the centre — 50 to 60 minutes. Turn the cake on to a wire rack and remove the paper. Leave to cool completely.

Meanwhile, make the topping. Put the curd cheese, yogurt and honey in a bowl and mix them together with a wooden spoon. Spread the top and sides of the cake evenly with the topping and score it with a fork. Press pumpkin seeds against the sides of the cake.

EDITOR'S NOTE: *Use bought pumpkin seeds: those from the centre of the pumpkin would be too damp. To brown the seeds, heat them in a heavy-bottomed pan, shaking constantly, for 1 to 2 minutes until the colour begins to change.*

Maple Pumpkin Tea Bread

Serves 12
Working time: about 30 minutes
Total time: about 5 hours

Calories **160**
Protein **4g**
Cholesterol **45mg**
Total fat **7g**
Saturated fat **2g**
Sodium **60mg**

10 cl	safflower oil	3½ fl oz
10 cl	maple syrup	3½ fl oz
2	eggs	2
175 g	plain flour	6 oz
½ tsp	bicarbonate of soda	½ tsp
½ tsp	ground cinnamon	½ tsp
¼ tsp	ground cloves	¼ tsp
¼ tsp	grated nutmeg	¼ tsp
¼ tsp	baking powder	¼ tsp
¼ litre	pumpkin purée	8 fl oz
60 g	raisins	2 oz
90 g	shelled macadamia or Brazil nuts, roughly chopped	3 oz

Preheat the oven to 180°C (350°F or Mark 4). Grease a 22 by 12 cm (9 by 5 inch) loaf tin. Line its base with greaseproof paper and grease the paper.

Whisk the oil, maple syrup and eggs together in a bowl until pale. Sift the flour into another bowl with the bicarbonate of soda, cinnamon, cloves, nutmeg and baking powder. Fold the flour mixture into the eggs and syrup and mix in the pumpkin purée, raisins and 60 g (2 oz) of the nuts.

Transfer the mixture to the prepared tin and level the surface. Sprinkle the remaining nuts on top and bake for 1 to 1¼ hours, until risen and firm to the touch. Leave in the tin for 10 minutes, then unmould on to a wire tray. Cool completely before removing the paper.

EDITOR'S NOTE: *To make the pumpkin purée, remove the seeds from a 600 g (1¼ lb) wedge of pumpkin. Wrap the wedge in foil. Bake the pumpkin in a preheated 180°C (350°F or Mark 4) oven for 45 minutes. With a spoon, scoop the flesh into a food processor or blender and process the pumpkin until smooth.*

2 *Piped lines of cream adorn a layered sponge enlivened with cognac; strawberries will complete the decoration at virtually no calorie cost.*

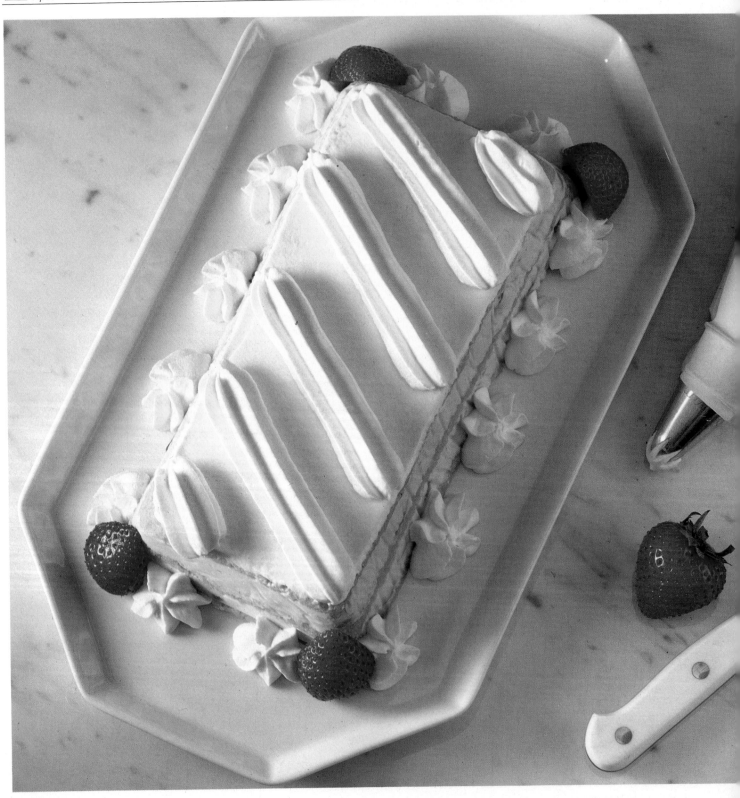

Stylish Presentations

Tiers of sponge and chocolate topped with caramel, a banana gateau with a lemon butter icing, a rum-flavoured savarin bordered with cream — such delights hardly spell austerity. Yet the special-occasion cakes in this chapter are no higher in calories and fat than the others in this book. The secret to the achievement lies in realizing most of the decoration with healthy ingredients such as low-fat cheese or fruit, then using small quantities of cream, butter, nuts and chocolate where they will be most appreciated.

A piping bag is a great asset to the health-conscious cook: it turns a mere 2 tablespoons of whipped cream into a scrolled border or a cluster of rosettes. Chocolate curls account for far less fat than a thick chocolate icing, yet look twice as professional. The marzipan ropes topping the fruit cake on page 72 require fewer almonds than would a solid layer. And where the decoration is more lavish, the recipes provide for a basic cake mixture that is not too rich.

Many of the cakes are made from *genoise*, a low-fat sponge aerated by whisking eggs and sugar over heat. This mixture, combined with flour, flavourings and sometimes a little melted butter, bakes to a very light sponge that would be dry on its own but which serves as an admirable foundation for assemblies. It can be layered with flavoured pastry cream or low-fat cheese, soaked in liqueur-spiked syrup, and topped with fruit or a skim of icing.

Another invaluable base — since it completely lacks fat — is meringue, made by whisking sugar into stiffly beaten egg whites. Meringue can be flavoured with cocoa, nuts or a spoonful of fruit purée. It can be piped into such intricate forms as the shell for a Pavlova *(recipe, page 91)* or it can be incorporated into a layered assembly such as the hazelnut and raspberry galette on page 92.

Genoise and meringue far from exhaust the scope of this chapter. There are cheesecakes and an ice cream cake, strawberry shortcake and a fruit-packed Christmas garland. As support for the recipes, techniques such as piping, lining tins and beating eggs and sugar over heat are shown on pages 12 to 19. Inspired by the recipes and guided by the step-by-step demonstrations, you can produce your own variations on the 24 decorative centrepieces in this chapter.

Parsnip and Orange Cake

THE GRATED PARSNIP IN THIS RECIPE PROVIDES MOISTURE AND A HINT OF CRUNCHINESS TO THE CAKE'S TEXTURE; THE DOMINANT FLAVOUR IS ORANGE.

Serves 14
Working time: about 30 minutes
Total time: about 4 hours

Calories **210**
Protein **5g**
Cholesterol **40mg**
Total fat **10g**
Saturated fat **2g**
Sodium **240mg**

125 g	polyunsaturated margarine	4 oz
125 g	brown sugar	4 oz
2 tbsp	malt extract	2 tbsp
1	orange, grated rind and juice only	1
3	eggs	3
275 g	wholemeal flour	9 oz
1 tbsp	baking powder	1 tbsp
250 g	parsnips, peeled and grated	8 oz
Orange topping		
90 g	medium-fat curd cheese	3 oz
2 tsp	clear honey	2 tsp
1	orange, rind only, half grated, half julienned and blanched (page 18)	1

Preheat the oven to 170°C (325°F or Mark 3). Grease a deep 20 cm (8 inch) round cake tin. Line the base with greaseproof paper and grease the paper.

Cream the margarine, sugar, malt extract and orange rind until fluffy. Beat in the eggs one at a time, adding 1 tablespoon of flour with each egg. Sift the remaining flour with the baking powder, adding the bran left in the sieve. Fold the flour, parsnips and orange juice into the batter.

Turn the batter into the prepared tin. Bake the cake for about 1¼ hours, until a skewer inserted into the centre comes out clean.

Loosen the cake from the sides of the tin; turn the cake out on to a wire rack and remove the lining paper. Turn the cake the right way up and leave it to cool completely before icing it.

To make the orange topping, beat the curd cheese, honey and grated orange rind together. Spread the mixture over the top of the cake and flute it with a palette knife. Sprinkle the orange julienne round the edge of the cake.

Banana Walnut Cake

Serves 14
Working time: about 40 minutes
Total time: about 4 hours

Calories **285**
Protein **4g**
Cholesterol **25mg**
Total fat **15g**
Saturated fat **3g**
Sodium **125mg**

125 g	plain flour	4 oz
4 tsp	baking powder	4 tsp
125 g	wholemeal flour	4 oz
150 g	light brown sugar	5 oz
75 g	shelled walnuts	2½ oz
125 g	carrots, finely grated	4 oz
175 g	peeled bananas, mashed	6 oz
1	egg	1
8 cl	safflower oil	3 fl oz
Lemon butter icing		
45 g	unsalted butter	1½ oz
45 g	medium-fat curd cheese	1½ oz
¼ tsp	grated lemon rind	¼ tsp
90 g	icing sugar	3 oz

Preheat the oven to 180°C (350°F or Mark 4). Line an 18 cm (7 inch) square cake tin with non-stick parchment paper.

Sift the plain flour and baking powder into a bowl and mix in the wholemeal flour and brown sugar. Finely chop 45 g (1½ oz) of the walnuts and stir them in, together with the carrots. Using a wooden spoon, beat the mashed bananas with the egg and oil in a separate bowl. Make a well in the centre of the dry ingredients, add the banana mixture and beat the batter until it is evenly blended.

Turn the batter into the tin, level the top and cook the cake for about 1 hour, until it is well browned and firm to the touch; a skewer inserted in the centre should come out clean. Turn the cake out on to a wire rack and leave it to cool with the paper still attached.

To make the lemon butter icing, beat the butter with a wooden spoon until soft, then beat in the curd cheese and lemon rind. Sift in enough icing sugar to give a spreading consistency. Remove the paper from the cake and turn the cake the right way up. Spread the icing over the top of the cake, swirling it with a round-bladed knife. Break the remaining walnuts into large pieces and sprinkle them over the icing.

EDITOR'S NOTE: *Two bananas weigh approximately 175 g (6 oz) when peeled.*

Strawberry Ring

Serves 14
Working time: about 30 minutes
Total time: about 2 hours

Calories **120**
Protein **2g**
Cholesterol **0mg**
Total fat **3g**
Saturated fat **0g**
Sodium **65mg**

125 g	plain flour	4 oz
2 tsp	baking powder	2 tsp
60 g	ground rice	2 oz
90 g	caster sugar	3 oz
1 tsp	pure vanilla extract	1 tsp
3 tbsp	safflower oil	3 tbsp
4	egg whites	4
250 g	strawberries, hulled	8 oz
1 tsp	arrowroot	1 tsp
30 g	icing sugar	1 oz
	strawberry leaves to garnish	

Preheat the oven to 180°C (350°F or Mark 4). Grease and lightly flour a 22 cm (9 inch) springform ring mould — preferably one with a pattern on its base.

Sift the flour and baking powder into a mixing bowl. Stir in the ground rice and caster sugar. In another bowl, whisk the vanilla extract with the oil and 4 tablespoons of water. Stir the liquids into the dry ingredients using a wooden spoon, then beat the mixture to create a smooth batter.

Whisk the egg whites in a clean bowl until they are stiff but not dry. With a large metal or plastic spoon, fold one third of the egg whites into the batter, followed by the remaining egg whites.

Pour the mixture into the prepared mould. Tap the mould against the work surface to level the mixture. Bake the cake in the centre of the oven until well risen and springy when touched in the centre — 20 to 25 minutes. Loosen the edges of the cake with a small palette knife, release the spring and turn the cake out on to a wire rack. Leave until completely cooled.

Sieve four of the strawberries into a small saucepan. Blend this purée with the arrowroot, then sift in the icing sugar. Bring the purée to the boil, stirring, and simmer it for 30 seconds, until it thickens. Leave the purée to cool completely.

Thinly slice half of the remaining strawberries and arrange them on the inner edge of the cake. Fill the hole in the centre with the whole strawberries and top them with a few strawberry leaves. Brush the top and sides of the ring with the strawberry purée.

Lime Savarin

Serves 12
Working time: about 1 hour
Total time: about 3 hours and 30 minutes

Calories **255**
Protein **4g**
Cholesterol **70mg**
Total fat **10g**
Saturated fat **5g**
Sodium **30mg**

20 g	fresh yeast, or 15 g (½ oz) dried yeast	¾ oz
5 tbsp	milk, tepid	5 tbsp
30 g	caster sugar	1 oz
90 g	strong plain flour	3 oz
90 g	wholemeal flour	3 oz
⅛ tsp	salt	⅛ tsp
2	eggs	2
60 g	unsalted butter, softened	2 oz
2	limes, freshly grated rind only	2
1	lime, halved vertically, each half cut into six slices	1
4 tbsp	apricot jam without added sugar	4 tbsp
6 tbsp	double cream, whipped	6 tbsp
Rum and lime syrup		
3 tbsp	fresh lime juice	3 tbsp
5 tbsp	clear honey	5 tbsp
2 tbsp	white rum	2 tbsp

In a large bowl, mix the fresh yeast with the milk, the sugar and 1 tablespoon of the plain flour, or reconstitute the dried yeast according to the manufacturer's instructions. Leave the yeast mixture in a warm place for about 10 minutes, until it is frothy. Then add the remaining plain flour to the bowl, together with the wholemeal flour, salt, eggs, butter and lime rind. Beat the ingredients together with a wooden spoon.

Grease a 20 cm (8 inch) ring mould and transfer the dough to the mould. Cover the dough with oiled plastic film and leave it to rise in a warm place for 30 to 40 minutes, until the mixture is about 2 cm (¾ inch) from the top of the mould. Meanwhile, preheat the oven to 200°C (400°F or Mark 6).

Bake the savarin for 25 to 30 minutes, until it is golden-brown and firm to the touch.

While the savarin is cooking, blanch the lime slices to reduce their bitterness: distribute them in a wide, shallow saucepan, pour boiling water over them, bring the water back to the boil and drain the slices. Set the slices aside. Put the lime juice and honey in the pan with 3 tablespoons of water. Bring the syrup to a simmer, put the lime slices back in the pan and poach them gently for 10 minutes. Remove them from the pan. Bring the syrup to the boil: the hotter it is when it goes on the cake, the more effectively it will soak in. Remove the pan from the heat and add the rum.

Unmould the savarin on to a large plate or tray and immediately spoon the hot syrup over it. Warm the apricot jam in a small saucepan. Sieve it and brush it over the surface of the savarin. Leave the savarin to cool, then transfer it to a serving dish. Arrange the lime slices round the cake's rim. (For some tastes, lime is too tart and serves simply as decoration.) Spoon the cream into a piping bag fitted with a medium star nozzle and pipe shells round the base of the savarin.

Semolina Fruit Cake

Serves 14
Working time: about 30 minutes
Total time: about 4 hours and 30 minutes

Calories **215**
Protein **4g**
Cholesterol **40mg**
Total fat **11g**
Saturated fat **3g**
Sodium **120mg**

125 g	polyunsaturated margarine	4 oz
125 g	soft brown sugar	4 oz
2	eggs	2
125 g	semolina	4 oz
60 g	plain flour	2 oz
1 tsp	baking powder	1 tsp
2 tbsp	skimmed milk	2 tbsp
60 g	mixed candied peel, chopped	2 oz
30 g	shelled hazelnuts, toasted and chopped	1 oz
125 g	currants	4 oz
Almond paste		
25 g	icing sugar	¾ oz
25 g	caster sugar	¾ oz
45 g	ground almonds	1½ oz
2 tsp	egg white, lightly whisked	2 tsp
½ tsp	lemon juice	½ tsp
½ tsp	cocoa powder	½ tsp

Preheat the oven to 180°C (350°F or Mark 4). Line an 18 cm (7 inch) square cake tin with non-stick parchment paper.

Cream the margarine and sugar together until very pale and fluffy. With a wooden spoon, beat in the eggs one at a time, following each with 1 tablespoon of the semolina. Sift the flour with the baking powder and add them to the mixture with the rest of the semolina and the milk. If necessary, add a few drops more milk to give a soft dropping consistency. Fold in the mixed peel, hazelnuts and currants. Turn the mixture into the prepared tin and level the top.

Cook the cake for about 1 hour, until it is firm to the touch and a skewer inserted in the centre comes out clean. Leave the cake in the tin for 5 minutes, then turn it out on to a wire rack. Leave it until cool before removing the lining paper.

To make the almond paste, sift the icing sugar into a bowl and mix in the caster sugar and almonds. Add the egg white and lemon juice. On a board sprinkled with icing sugar, knead the paste lightly until smooth.

Divide the almond paste in half and knead the cocoa into one portion. Roll out the paste into several long cylinders about 5 mm (¼ inch) in diameter. Twist each brown cylinder with a white one to make a rope. Lay strips of almond rope diagonally across the cake at about 4 cm (1½ inch) intervals and trim the edges off neatly. The almond ropes should stick to the cake by themselves if lightly pressed, but if not, attach them with dabs of honey.

EDITOR'S NOTE: *To toast hazelnuts, place them on a baking sheet in a 180°C (350°F or Mark 4) oven for 10 minutes.*

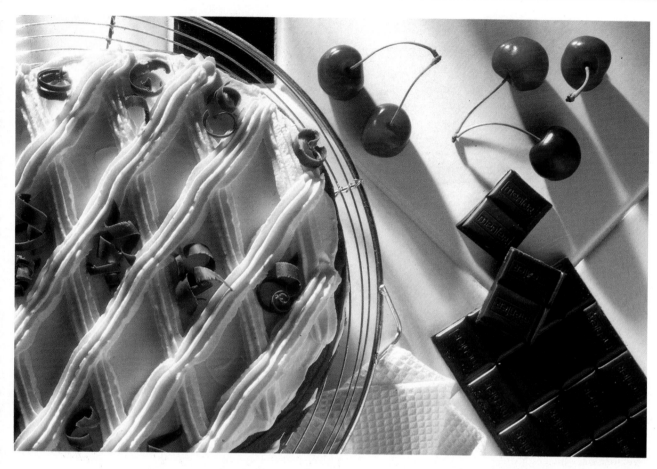

Black Cherry Chocolate Gateau

Serves 12
Working time: about 50 minutes
Total time: about 3 hours

Calories **140**
Protein **5g**
Cholesterol **60mg**
Total fat **5g**
Saturated fat **3g**
Sodium **80mg**

500 g	black cherries	1 lb
1½ tsp	powdered gelatine	1½ tsp
3	eggs	3
100 g	caster sugar	3½ oz
90 g	plain flour	3 oz
15 g	cocoa powder	½ oz
½ tsp	baking powder	½ tsp
3 tbsp	kirsch or brandy	3 tbsp
175 g	medium-fat soft cheese	6 oz
5 tbsp	whipping cream	5 tbsp
15 g	chocolate curls (page 19)	½ oz

Preheat the oven to 190°C (375°F or Mark 5). Grease a round cake tin about 21 cm (8½ inches) in diameter and line it with non-stick parchment paper.

Set aside 13 or 14 perfect cherries to decorate the cake. Simmer the rest very gently in 15 cl (¼ pint) of water until they are tender but still intact — 7 to 8 minutes. Strain the liquid into a measuring jug and, if necessary, make up the volume to 175 cl (6 fl oz) with water. Put 1 tablespoon of water in a small bowl and stand it in a pan of gently simmering water. Add the gelatine. When the gelatine has dissolved, stir it into the cherry liquid. Halve the cherries, discarding the stones, and add them to the liquid. Leave the liquid to cool, then refrigerate it until it sets — about 2 hours.

Meanwhile, put the eggs and all but 2 teaspoons of the sugar in a large bowl resting over a pan of hot, but not boiling, water. Whisk by hand or with an electric mixer until the eggs are thick and very pale. Remove the bowl from the heat and continue to whisk until the whisk leaves a heavy trail when lifted (page 12). Sift the flour, cocoa and baking powder together twice and fold them quickly and evenly through the egg mixture with a metal spoon. Turn the batter into the prepared tin and level the top. Cook for 20 to 25 minutes, until well risen and firm to the touch. Turn the sponge out on to a wire rack, loosen the lining paper but do not remove it and leave the sponge to cool.

To assemble the gateau, cut the sponge in half horizontally and place the bottom half on a serving plate. Sprinkle it with the kirsch. Mix the soft cheese with the remaining sugar and spread half of it over the sponge. Stir the cherry jelly, and spread it and the stewed cherries evenly over the cheese. Top the cherries with the second layer of sponge. Spread its top with the remaining cheese mixture.

Whip the cream and spoon it into a piping bag fitted with a small star nozzle. Pipe a lattice of cream on to the cake. Arrange the chocolate curls and reserved cherries in the gaps. Chill the cake until it is served.

Apricot Tricorn

Serves 12
Working time: about 45 minutes
Total time: about 3 hours

Calories **170**
Protein **4g**
Cholesterol **70mg**
Total fat **7g**
Saturated fat **2g**
Sodium **60mg**

3	eggs	3
130 g	caster sugar	4¼ oz
90 g	plain flour	3 oz
1	lemon, finely grated rind only	1
350 g	fresh apricots	12 oz
250 g	cooking apples, peeled, cored and sliced	8 oz
2 tbsp	brandy	2 tbsp
125 g	medium-fat soft cheese	4 oz
6 tbsp	whipping cream	6 tbsp
45 g	flaked almonds, lightly toasted	1½ oz

Preheat the oven to 190°C (375°F or Mark 5). Grease a rectangular tin approximately 28 by 18 by 4 cm (11 by 7 by 1½ inches). Line it with greaseproof paper, and grease the paper.

In a bowl set over a pan of hot, but not boiling, water, whisk the eggs with 90 g (3 oz) of the sugar, either by hand or with an electric whisk or beater, until the eggs are thick and very pale. Remove the bowl from the heat and continue whisking until the whisk leaves a heavy trail when lifted *(page 12)*. Sift the flour twice and fold it quickly and evenly through the mixture, together with the lemon rind. Turn the batter into the prepared tin and level the top. Bake the sponge for 20 to 25 minutes until well risen and firm to the touch. Turn it out on to a wire rack, loosen the lining paper but do not remove it and leave the sponge until cold.

For the filling, halve and stone the apricots. Simmer them gently in a wide saucepan in 25 cl (8 fl oz) of water until they are tender — about 10 minutes. Strain the liquid, skin the apricots and reserve 10 halves for decoration. Return the remaining apricots to the pan with the apples and 1 tablespoon of the apricot liquid. Cover the pan and stew the fruit gently until the apples are soft — about 5 minutes. Add 30 g (1 oz) of the remaining sugar to the fruit and leave it to cool.

Cut across the sponge between the centre of the long side and first one, then the other, opposite corner. The two cuts yield one large sponge triangle, and two smaller triangles that together are the same size as the large one. Put the two smaller pieces of sponge on a board to form a triangle the same shape as the large piece of sponge. Lay the large sponge on top and trim the sponges to exactly the same dimensions.

Transfer the two smaller sponges to a serving dish and sprinkle them with the brandy. Spread them with the apple and apricot mixture, then top them with the large sponge triangle.

Beat the soft cheese with the remaining 10 g (¼ oz) of sugar. Whip the cream until it is stiff and fold 2 tablespoons into the cheese mixture. Mask the top and sides of the gateau with the cheese mixture. Press the toasted almonds against the sides of the gateau. Spoon the remaining cream into a piping bag fitted with a medium star nozzle and pipe a row of shells along two edges of the gateau. Arrange the reserved apricot halves on top of the gateau and pipe cream shells along the third border.

EDITOR'S NOTE: *To toast flaked almonds, put them under the grill for 2 minutes or until they become golden; turn or shake them constantly.*

Piña Colada Gateau

WITH ITS FLAVOURINGS OF COCONUT, PINEAPPLE AND RUM,
THIS CAKE CONTAINS ALL THE INGREDIENTS OF THE CARIBBEAN
COCKTAIL PIÑA COLADA.

Serves 12
Working time: about 45 minutes
Total time: about 2 hours and 45 minutes

Calories **235**
Protein **4g**
Cholesterol **80mg**
Total fat **13g**
Saturated fat **9g**
Sodium **130mg**

90 g	unsalted butter	3 oz
90 g	caster sugar	3 oz
2	eggs, lightly beaten	2
90 g	plain flour	3 oz
1 tsp	baking powder	1 tsp
60 g	desiccated coconut	2 oz
Pineapple and rum custard		
2 tbsp	plain flour	2 tbsp
2 tbsp	cornflour	2 tbsp
30 g	caster sugar	1 oz
1	egg yolk	1
30 cl	skimmed milk	½ pint
125 g	fresh pineapple flesh, finely chopped	4 oz
1 tbsp	dark rum	1 tbsp
30 g	desiccated coconut	1 oz

Preheat the oven to 180°C (350°F or Mark 4). Grease two 20 cm (8 inch) round sandwich tins. Line the bases with greaseproof paper and grease the paper.

Cream the butter and sugar together in a large bowl until they are pale and fluffy. Beat the eggs into the creamed butter with a wooden spoon a little at a time. Sift the flour and baking powder together into the egg mixture, and add the desiccated coconut. Fold in the flour and coconut with a metal spoon.

Divide the mixture equally between the prepared tins, and level the surfaces. Bake the sponges for about 20 minutes, until they are risen and firm to the touch. Turn them out on to a wire rack and leave them to cool with the lining paper still attached.

Meanwhile, make the pineapple and rum custard. Using a wooden spoon, mix together the flour, corn-flour, sugar and egg yolk with half of the milk in a large bowl. Bring the remaining milk to the boil in a saucepan and pour it over the egg mixture, stirring well. Return the custard to the pan and cook it over gentle heat, stirring all the time, until it has thickened enough to leave a trail. Pour the custard into a bowl to cool and cover it closely with plastic film to prevent a skin from forming.

Pour half of the custard from the bowl in which it has cooled into a second bowl. Add the pineapple to one bowl of custard and the rum to the other. Remove the lining paper from the sponges and sandwich them together with the pineapple custard. Coat the top and sides of the cake with the rum custard. Scatter desiccated coconut evenly over the rum custard.

Cool Caribbean Cake

Serves 10
Working time: about 40 minutes
Total time: about 5 hours

Calories **180**
Protein **4g**
Cholesterol **5mg**
Total fat **5g**
Saturated fat **2g**
Sodium **95mg**

60 g	plain chocolate	2 oz
2 tsp	clear honey	2 tsp
15 g	unsalted butter	½ oz
125 g	breakfast wheat flakes	4 oz
2 tbsp	whipped cream	2 tbsp
1 tbsp	coconut flakes	1 tbsp
Coconut ice cream		
60 g	creamed coconut	2 oz
2 tbsp	clear honey	2 tbsp
15 cl	plain low-fat yogurt	¼ pint
1	egg white	1
Mango ice cream		
2	mangoes, peeled and chopped	2
4 tbsp	fresh orange juice	4 tbsp
2 tbsp	clear honey	2 tbsp
15 cl	plain low-fat yogurt	¼ pint
1	egg white	1

Line an 18 cm (7 inch) round cake tin with non-stick parchment paper. Half-fill a small saucepan with water and bring it to the boil; remove it from the heat. Put the chocolate, honey and butter in a bowl over the saucepan of hot water. Stir occasionally until the chocolate and butter have melted. Add the wheat flakes and stir to coat them with the chocolate mixture. Spread the chocolate wheat flakes in the base of the prepared tin. Level the layer with the back of a spoon and press it well down. Put the tin in the freezer.

To make the coconut ice cream, put 15 cl (¼ pint) of water in a small saucepan and bring it to the boil. Remove the water from the heat and stir in the creamed coconut and the honey. Leave the blend to cool completely, then stir in the yogurt and pour the mixture into a shallow plastic container. Place the coconut ice cream in the freezer and leave it until firm but not frozen hard — about 1 hour.

Meanwhile, make the mango ice cream. Purée the mangoes with the orange juice, honey and yogurt in a blender or food processor. Pour the purée into a shallow plastic container and place it in the freezer. Leave it until firm but not frozen hard — 1 to 2 hours.

Remove the coconut ice cream from the freezer. To break down the crystals, put the ice cream in a bowl and whisk it until smooth, or blend it in a food processor. Whisk the egg white until stiff in a separate bowl, then whisk the egg white into the ice cream. Pour the ice cream over the chocolate wheat flakes and freeze the two layers until firm but not frozen hard.

When the coconut layer is almost set, remove the ▶

mango ice cream from the freezer. Put it in a bowl and whisk it until smooth, or blend it in a food processor. Whisk the egg white until stiff in a separate bowl, then whisk the egg white into the ice cream. Pour the mango ice cream on top of the frozen layers of coconut ice cream and chocolate flakes and return the cake to the freezer until frozen — about 2 hours.

About 40 minutes before serving the cake, dip the base of the tin in warm water for a second and turn the cake out. Peel off the parchment paper and turn the cake on to a plate. Spoon the whipped cream into a piping bag fitted with a small star nozzle. Pipe whirls of cream round the top edge of the cake and decorate the cake with the coconut flakes. Leave the cake in the refrigerator to soften for 30 minutes before serving it.

EDITOR'S NOTE: *If precooked breakfast wheat flakes are not available, substitute raw wheat flakes. Before stirring them into the chocolate mixture, toast them for 2 to 3 minutes under a medium grill. Creamed coconut, available in many supermarkets, is prepared from the puréed flesh of the nut.*

Strawberry Shortcake

Serves 10
Working time: about 45 minutes
Total time: about 2 hours and 30 minutes

Calories **220**
Protein **5g**
Cholesterol **25mg**
Total fat **11g**
Saturated fat **4g**
Sodium **305mg**

150 g	plain flour	5 oz
60 g	ground almonds	2 oz
3 tbsp	caster sugar	3 tbsp
1 tbsp	baking powder	1 tbsp
45 g	unsalted butter	1½ oz
5 tbsp	buttermilk	5 tbsp
15 g	flaked almonds	½ oz
Strawberry filling		
250 g	strawberries, one reserved, the rest hulled and chopped	8 oz
4 tbsp	claret or port	4 tbsp
125 g	cottage cheese, sieved	4 oz
4 tbsp	double cream, whipped	4 tbsp
1 tbsp	caster sugar	1 tbsp
	icing sugar to decorate	

Preheat the oven to 200°C (400°F or Mark 6). Add the chopped strawberries for the filling to the claret and leave them to macerate.

Sift the flour, ground almonds, sugar and baking powder together into a bowl. Rub in the butter until the mixture resembles fine crumbs. Stir in about 4 tablespoons of the buttermilk — enough to give a soft dough. Knead the dough gently on a lightly floured surface, then press it out to an 18 cm (7 inch) round. Place the round on a non-stick baking sheet.

With a knife, mark the top of the dough into 10 sections. Brush the top with buttermilk and sprinkle it with the almonds. Bake the shortcake for about 25 minutes, until it is crisp and golden. Turn it out to cool on a wire rack. When the shortcake is cold, split it in half horizontally and cut the top into the 10 sections.

To make the strawberry filling, mix the cottage cheese with the whipped cream and caster sugar. Strain the juice from the macerated strawberries and keep it for another use; then fold the strawberries into the cream mixture.

Just before serving the cake, spread the strawberry cream over the base of the shortcake. Cover it with the 10 top sections and dust them lightly with icing sugar. Slice the reserved strawberry and arrange the slices in the centre of the cake.

Strawberry Cognac Layer Cake

Serves 10
Working time: about 1 hour
Total time: about 10 hours

Calories **175**
Protein **8g**
Cholesterol **60mg**
Total fat **7g**
Saturated fat **3g**
Sodium **145mg**

2	eggs	2
1	egg white	1
90 g	vanilla-flavoured caster sugar	3 oz
90 g	plain flour	3 oz
3 tbsp	cognac	3 tbsp
5 tbsp	skimmed milk	5 tbsp
6 tbsp	whipping cream	6 tbsp
	Strawberry filling	
250 g	cottage cheese, sieved	8 oz
3 tbsp	skimmed milk	3 tbsp
2 tbsp	clear honey	2 tbsp
1	lemon, grated rind only	1
1 tbsp	fresh lemon juice	1 tbsp
1½ tsp	powdered gelatine	1½ tsp
250 g	strawberries	8 oz

Preheat the oven to 190°C (375°F or Mark 5). Line a loaf tin approximately 22 by 11 cm (9 by 4½ inches) and a shallow rectangular tin approximately 32 by 22 cm (13 by 9 inches) with non-stick parchment paper.

Put the eggs, egg white and sugar in a bowl set over a pan of gently simmering water. Whisk with a hand whisk or electric beater until the mixture is very thick and the whisk leaves a heavy trail when lifted *(page 12)*. Remove the mixture from the heat and whisk it until it is cool. Sift the flour twice and fold it quickly and evenly into the egg mixture with a metal spoon. Turn the batter into the shallow rectangular tin and level the top. Cook the sponge for 12 to 15 minutes, until well risen and firm to the touch. Turn it out on to a wire rack; leave until cold, then peel off the paper.

Meanwhile, make the filling. Put the cottage cheese, milk, honey and lemon rind in a bowl and beat them with a wooden spoon. Put the lemon juice in a small bowl and stand it in a pan of gently simmering water, then add the gelatine and leave it to dissolve. Stir the gelatine into the cheese mixture. Slice half the strawberries and add them to the mixture.

Cut lengthwise and across the rectangle of sponge to obtain a piece that fits the base of the loaf tin. Set it in position. Combine the cognac and the 5 tablespoons of milk and pour 3 tablespoons over the cake in the tin. When the strawberry-cheese mixture begins to thicken, spoon half into the loaf tin. Cut a second piece of sponge, slightly larger than the first, and use it to cover the strawberry-cheese mixture. Soak the sponge with half of the remaining cognac and milk, and spoon in the rest of the strawberry-cheese mixture. From the piece of sponge that remains, cut enough to cover the second strawberry-cheese layer. Moisten it with the rest of the cognac and milk. Cover the cake with non-stick parchment paper and a rectangle of cardboard to distribute weight. Set a 500 g to 1 kg (1 to 2 lb) weight on the cake and refrigerate overnight; long chilling makes it firm and easy to slice.

Just before serving the cake, turn it out and peel off the paper. Whip the cream until stiff and spread 1 tablespoon over the cake. Spoon the remainder into a piping bag fitted with a large star nozzle. Pipe diagonal lines across the cake top, stars round the base. Slice or halve the remaining strawberries; arrange them round the base and between the lines of cream.

Dobostorte

NAMED AFTER ITS INVENTOR JOZSEF C. DOBOS, A FAMOUS
HUNGARIAN PATISSIER, THIS CAKE CONSISTS OF FATLESS SPONGE
LAYERED WITH CHOCOLATE PASTRY CREAM AND TOPPED WITH
CARAMEL. TO MAKE THE THIN, DELICATE SHEETS OF SPONGE, THE
BATTER IS SPREAD OUT ON MARKED PAPER AND THE SPONGES ARE
TRIMMED TO SHAPE AFTER BAKING. IN THIS VERSION, THE
CHOCOLATE PASTRY CREAM IS CONSIDERABLY LESS RICH THAN IN
THE ORIGINAL CREATION.

Serves 12
Working time: about 1 hour
Total time: about 2 hours and 30 minutes

Calories **175**
Protein **4g**
Cholesterol **65mg**
Total fat **5g**
Saturated fat **2g**
Sodium **35mg**

3	eggs	3
125 g	vanilla-flavoured caster sugar	4 oz
125 g	plain flour	4 oz
90 g	granulated sugar	3 oz
30 cl	chocolate-flavoured pastry cream (page 16)	½ pint
5 tbsp	whipping cream	5 tbsp
12	hazelnuts, shelled, toasted and skinned	12

Preheat the oven to 190°C (375°F or Mark 5). Draw two
25 by 11 cm (10 by 4½ inch) rectangles on each of two
sheets of non-stick parchment paper. Place each
sheet, marked side down, on a baking sheet.

Put the eggs and vanilla-flavoured sugar in a bowl
set over a pan of gently simmering water. Whisk the
mixture for about 10 minutes with a hand or electric
whisk until the eggs are very thick and creamy and the
whisk leaves a heavy trail when lifted *(page 12)*.
Remove the bowl from the heat and continue whisking
the mixture until it is cool. Sift the flour twice and fold it

quickly and evenly into the egg mixture. Spoon the
mixture into the four marked rectangles and spread it
out evenly. Cook the sponges for 10 to 12 minutes,
until they are firm and a pale golden-brown.

The sponges spread a little during cooking; while
they are still warm, trim them with a serrated knife to
the dimensions marked on the paper. Transfer the
sponges, still on the paper, to a wire rack to cool.

Select the smoothest sponge for the torte's top
layer, but leave it on the paper. Put the granulated
sugar in a small heavy-bottomed saucepan and heat
gently, without stirring, until the sugar melts and turns
golden. Pour the caramel quickly over the chosen
sponge and spread it with a knife to the edge of the
sponge. Before it sets, oil a heavy knife and mark a
cutting line lengthwise and six cutting lines across the
cake, giving 12 portions. Leave the caramel to harden.

To assemble the Dobostorte, peel one sponge layer
off the paper and place it on a serving dish. Spread the
sponge with one third of the chocolate pastry cream.
Cover the chocolate layer with a second layer of
sponge, more pastry cream, then a third layer of
sponge, the remaining chocolate pastry cream and
finally the caramel sponge layer. Whip the cream stiffly
and spoon it into a piping bag fitted with a large star
nozzle. Pipe a whirl of cream in the centre of each
marked portion and top each cream whirl with a
toasted hazelnut. Chill the Dobostorte until it is served.

EDITOR'S NOTE: *To toast and skin hazelnuts, place them on a
baking sheet in a preheated 180°C (350°F or Mark 4) oven for
10 minutes. Enfold them in a towel and roll them to and fro to
loosen the skins.*

Layered Marron and Orange Gateau

Serves 10
Working time: about 30 minutes
Total time: about 2 hours and 30 minutes

Calories **230**
Protein **5g**
Cholesterol **50mg**
Total fat **7g**
Saturated fat **2g**
Sodium **100mg**

125 g	brown flour	4 oz
1½ tsp	baking powder	1½ tsp
90 g	light brown sugar	3 oz
2 tbsp	safflower oil	2 tbsp
2	eggs, yolks and whites separated	2
1 tsp	grated orange rind	1 tsp
45 g	shelled hazelnuts, toasted and finely chopped	1½ oz
1	orange, skin and pith sliced off, flesh cut into segments (page 14)	1
Orange chestnut filling		
450 g	chestnut purée	15 oz
1	orange, grated rind only	1
4 tbsp	plain low-fat yogurt	4 tbsp
1 tbsp	clear honey	1 tbsp

Preheat the oven to 180°C (350°F or Mark 4). Grease a deep 20 cm (8 inch) cake tin and line its base with greaseproof paper. Grease and lightly flour the paper.

Sift the flour and baking powder together into a mixing bowl and stir in the sugar. Whisk the oil in a small bowl with the egg yolks, the orange rind and 3 tablespoons of water. Stir the liquid into the flour mix-ture, then beat with a wooden spoon to make a smooth, glossy batter. In another bowl, whisk the egg whites until stiff but not dry. Add one third of the whites to the batter and fold them in using a spatula or large metal or plastic spoon. Fold in the remaining whites and pour the mixture into the prepared tin. Tap the tin on the work surface to level the mixture.

Bake the cake in the centre of the oven for 25 to 30 minutes, until well risen, lightly browned and springy when touched in the centre. Loosen the edges of the cake with a palette knife and turn it out of the tin on to a wire rack. Remove the lining paper and leave the cake until it has cooled completely.

To make the filling, beat the chestnut purée, orange rind, yogurt and honey in a bowl with a wooden spoon until smooth. Spoon 2 tablespoons of the filling into a piping bag fitted with a small star nozzle.

Cut the cake into three layers. Put the base layer on a plate and spread its top surface with one quarter of the remaining filling. Stack and spread the other layers in the same way and spread the final quarter of the filling over the sides of the cake. Press the chopped hazelnuts against the sides of the cake to coat them evenly. Arrange the orange segments radiating out-wards from the centre of the cake. Pipe stars round the top of the cake and a rosette in the centre.

EDITOR'S NOTE: *To obtain 450 g (15 oz) chestnut purée from fresh chestnuts, slit about 1 kg (2 lb) of chestnuts down one side, parboil them for 1 to 2 minutes, shell and peel them. Simmer the chestnuts for about 20 minutes in water, until they are tender. Drain and sieve them. To toast hazelnuts, put them on a baking sheet in a preheated 180°C (350°F or Mark 4) oven for 10 minutes.*

Pear and Port Wine Cheesecake

Serves 12
Working time: about 40 minutes
Total time: about 2 hours and 30 minutes

Calories **200**
Protein **4g**
Cholesterol **35mg**
Total fat **10g**
Saturated fat **3g**
Sodium **195mg**

175 g	digestive biscuits, crushed	6 oz
60 g	unsalted butter, melted	2 oz
1 tsp	ground cinnamon	1 tsp
250 g	medium-fat curd cheese	8 oz
60 g	caster sugar	2 oz
1 tsp	finely grated lemon rind	1 tsp
1	egg	1
3	large pears	3
1 tbsp	fresh lemon juice	1 tbsp
6 tbsp	port	6 tbsp
1 tbsp	currants	1 tbsp
1 tsp	arrowroot	1 tsp

Preheat the oven to 180°C (350°F or Mark 4). In a bowl, mix the biscuit crumbs with the butter and cinnamon.

Spread the mixture over the bottom of a 22 cm (9 inch) round springform cake tin and press lightly. Bake the biscuit base for 15 minutes, then leave it to cool.

With a wooden spoon, beat together the curd cheese, sugar, lemon rind and egg. Peel and core the pears. Slice them thinly and sprinkle the slices with lemon juice. Cover the biscuit base with the cheese mixture, then arrange the pear slices on top in an overlapping pattern. Bake the cheesecake for about 35 minutes until it is set. Leave the cake to cool in the tin, then transfer it to a serving plate.

Put the port, currants and arrowroot in a small pan. Cook them, stirring, over gentle heat for 1 minute, until the liquid thickens. Leave it for a minute or two to cool; spoon the mixture over the cake to glaze the pears.

Redcurrant and Blackcurrant Cheesecake

Serves 12
Working time: about 30 minutes
Total time: about 3 hours

Calories **195**
Protein **7g**
Cholesterol **30mg**
Total fat **10g**
Saturated fat **3g**
Sodium **180mg**

90 g	brown flour	3 oz
30 g	wholemeal semolina	1 oz
1 tsp	baking powder	1 tsp
45 g	unsalted butter	1½ oz
3 tbsp	clear honey	3 tbsp
500 g	medium-fat curd cheese	1 lb
15 cl	plain low-fat yogurt	¼ pint
1 tsp	pure vanilla extract	1 tsp
1	egg	1
250 g	redcurrants, picked over and stemmed	8 oz
250 g	blackcurrants, picked over and stemmed	8 oz
60 g	caster sugar	2 oz
4 tsp	arrowroot	4 tsp

Preheat the oven to 180°C (350°F or Mark 4). Grease an 18 cm (7 inch) loose-based square cake tin.

To make the shortcake base, sift the brown flour, semolina and baking powder into a bowl. Rub in the butter with your fingertips until the mixture resembles breadcrumbs. Using a fork, stir in 1 tablespoon of the honey and 2 teaspoons of cold water. Knead the dough on a lightly floured surface, then roll it out and cut it to fit the cake tin. Lower the dough into the tin and press it well against the base and sides. Prick the dough with a fork and bake it for 10 minutes. Remove it from the oven and reduce the oven temperature to 150°C (300°F or Mark 2).

Meanwhile, beat the curd cheese, yogurt, remaining honey and vanilla extract in a mixing bowl with a wooden spoon. Add the egg and beat the mixture until smooth. Pour the mixture into the cake tin, then bake the cheesecake until the filling has set — about 1 hour. Let it cool in the tin, then transfer it to a plate.

While the cheesecake cooks, put the redcurrants and blackcurrants in separate saucepans and distribute the caster sugar between the two pans. Cook the currants very gently for 2 minutes, shaking the pans occasionally, until the currants are softened but still whole. Strain the juice from the blackcurrants through a nylon sieve. Return the juice to the pan and put the fruit in a bowl. Strain the redcurrant juice through a clean nylon sieve; return the juice to the redcurrant pan and put the redcurrants in a second bowl.

Blend the arrowroot with 2 tablespoons of water, then stir half into each saucepan. Bring both pans of juice to the boil, stirring, and cook for 1 minute. Stir the thickened redcurrant juice gently into the redcurrants and the thickened blackcurrant juice into the blackcurrants. Chill the currants until the cheesecake has cooled. Arrange bands of the redcurrants and blackcurrants on top of the cheesecake.

EDITOR'S NOTE: *The blackcurrants can be replaced by blueberries; ½ teaspoon of cinnamon or ¼ teaspoon of mace can be added to the dough for the base.*

Apricot Gooseberry Cheese Ring

Serves 12
Working time: about 30 minutes
Total time: about 2 hours and 40 minutes

Calories **180**
Protein **8g**
Cholesterol **0mg**
Total fat **8g**
Saturated fat **1g**
Sodium **20mg**

250 g	dried apricots	8 oz
250 g	gooseberries, topped and tailed	8 oz
250 g	quark	8 oz
15 cl	plain low-fat yogurt	¼ pint
15 g	powdered gelatine	½ oz
125 g	fresh apricots, stoned and sliced	4 oz
Honey crunch base		
150 g	rolled oats	5 oz
15 g	sesame seeds	½ oz
15 g	shelled hazelnuts, chopped	½ oz
4 tbsp	safflower oil	4 tbsp
2 tbsp	clear honey	2 tbsp

Put the dried apricots in a saucepan with 30 cl (½ pint) of water. Bring the water to the boil and simmer the apricots until they are tender — 15 to 20 minutes. Purée them in a blender or food processor, then transfer them to a bowl. Simmer the gooseberries in 2 tablespoons of water until tender — 8 to 10 minutes. Sieve the gooseberries into the apricot purée.

Put the quark and yogurt in another bowl and beat them with a wooden spoon until smooth. Gradually beat in the fruit purée. Blend the gelatine with 3 tablespoons of water in a small bowl; stand the bowl in a saucepan of hot water and stir occasionally until the gelatine has dissolved. Pour the gelatine into the fruit mixture, stirring continuously; beat until the mixture is well blended. Pour the mixture into a 1.5 litre (2½ pint) ring mould and leave it in a cool place until the gelatine is just beginning to set — about 1 hour.

To make the honey crunch base, mix the oats, sesame seeds and hazelnuts in a bowl. Add the safflower oil and stir well to coat the dry ingredients. Spread the oat mixture in a 32 by 22 cm (13 by 9 inch) baking tin and brown it under a medium grill for 15 minutes, turning the cereal once. Heat the honey in a saucepan. When it boils, stir in the oat mixture. Let the cereal cool for 5 minutes, then spoon it on to the cheesecake's surface; smooth the top with a small palette knife and press down gently.

Refrigerate the cheesecake until firm — about 1 hour. Dip the mould in hand-hot water to loosen the cheesecake. Cover the mould with the serving plate, invert the cheesecake on to the plate and remove the mould carefully. Arrange the sliced apricots round the top of the cheesecake.

EDITOR'S NOTE: *The gooseberries can be replaced by other fruit such as apples or pears.*

Muesli Cheese Tart

Serves 12
Working time: about 30 minutes
Total time: about 2 hours

Calories **170**
Protein **8g**
Cholesterol **35mg**
Total fat **8g**
Saturated **3g**
Sodium **80mg**

350 g	low-fat soft cheese	12 oz
1 tbsp	clear honey	1 tbsp
1	egg	1
½ tsp	pure vanilla extract	½ tsp
20 cl	plain low-fat yogurt	7 fl oz
2 tbsp	toasted and chopped shelled hazelnuts	2 tbsp
1	lime, rind only, julienned and blanched (page 18)	1

Hazelnut muesli base

3 tbsp	clear honey	3 tbsp
30 g	unsalted butter	1 oz
90 g	rolled oats	3 oz
30 g	raisins	1 oz
1 tbsp	toasted and chopped shelled hazelnuts	1 tbsp
1 tbsp	chopped dried apples	1 tbsp

Preheat the oven to 170°C (325°F or Mark 3). Grease a 35 by 11 cm (14 by 4½ inch) loose-based plain or fluted oblong tart tin.

To make the muesli base, heat the honey and butter in a saucepan, stirring occasionally. When the butter has melted, remove the pan from the heat and stir in the oats, raisins, hazelnuts and dried apples. Spread the muesli mixture over the base of the tin and level the top with a small palette knife.

Put the soft cheese, honey, egg and vanilla extract in a mixing bowl with all but 3 tablespoons of the yogurt. Mix the ingredients together with a wooden spoon, then beat them until smooth. Spoon the mixture over the muesli base and level the top with a small palette knife. Bake the cheesecake in the centre of the oven until the filling feels firm when touched in the centre — 20 to 25 minutes.

Remove the cake from the oven and spread the remaining yogurt over the top. Return the cake to the oven for 5 minutes, until the topping has set.

Let the cake cool in the tin. When it reaches room temperature, transfer it to a plate, sprinkle hazelnuts along both sides of the cake and strew the lime julienne down the middle.

EDITOR'S NOTE: *To toast hazelnuts, put them on a baking sheet in a preheated 180°C (350°F or Mark 4) oven for 10 minutes.*

Valentine Gateau

Serves 12
Working time: about 1 hour
Total time: about 3 hours

Calories **205**
Protein **4g**
Cholesterol **65mg**
Total fat **4g**
Saturated fat **1g**
Sodium **50mg**

3	eggs	3
90 g	caster sugar	3 oz
90 g	plain flour	3 oz
½ tsp	baking powder	½ tsp
1½ tsp	instant coffee powder	1½ tsp
30 cl	pastry cream (page 16)	½ pint
250 g	fresh raspberries, or frozen raspberries, thawed	8 oz
4	sugar-frosted rose petals (page 18)	4
Patterned coffee icing		
150 g	icing sugar	5 oz
1 tsp	very strong black coffee	1 tsp
30 g	plain chocolate	1 oz

Preheat the oven to 190°C (375°F or Mark 5). Grease a heart-shaped cake tin approximately 20 cm (8 inches) across at the widest part. Line the tin with non-stick parchment paper.

Using a hand or electric whisk, whisk the eggs and sugar together in a bowl set over a pan of simmering water for about 10 minutes — until the mixture is very thick and creamy and the whisk leaves a heavy trail when lifted (page 12). Remove the bowl from the heat and whisk the mixture until it is cool. Sift the flour, baking powder and coffee powder together twice, then fold them lightly and evenly into the mixture with a metal spoon. Turn the mixture into the prepared tin and level the top. Cook the sponge for about 25 minutes, until well risen and firm to the touch. Turn it out on to a wire rack, loosen the lining paper but do not remove it and leave the sponge until cool.

Cut the cake in half horizontally. Spread the lower half with the pastry cream and then cover it with the raspberries. Place the top half of the cake in position.

To make the coffee glacé icing, sift the icing sugar into a bowl and add the black coffee and about 3 teaspoons of hot water — enough to give a thick, smooth coating consistency. Pour the icing over the top of the cake and spread it evenly almost to the edge using a wet palette knife. Leave the icing to set.

When the icing is firm, melt the chocolate and spoon it into a greaseproof paper icing bag (page 17). Cut off the bag's tip and pipe a lacy line back and forth over the coffee icing. Leave the chocolate to set. Complete the decoration with the sugar-frosted rose petals.

A Piped Roulade and its Decoration

MAKING MERINGUE MUSHROOMS. To make the mushroom stalks, pipe 10 pointed rosettes 1.5 cm (½ inch) in diameter, spaced well apart on the parchment paper. To make the mushroom caps, pipe 10 flatter rosettes 2.5 cm (1 inch) in diameter.

PIPING THE ROULADE BATTER. Pipe the chocolate-flavoured batter in straight lines across the prepared tin. Each line should touch its neighbours, to create a continuous ridged sheet.

Yule Log

YULE LOG RECIPES USUALLY PRESCRIBE A SPONGE ROULADE
COVERED WITH CHOCOLATE BUTTER ICING. THIS LOW-FAT VERSION
IS CONSTRUCTED FROM A CHOCOLATE-FLAVOURED EGG-WHITE
BATTER WITH A CHESTNUT FILLING.

Serves 12
Working time: about 1 hour
Total time: about 2 hours and 30 minutes

Calories **175**
Protein **2g**
Cholesterol **5mg**
Total fat **4g**
Saturated fat **2g**
Sodium **25mg**

6	egg whites	6
190 g	caster sugar	6½ oz
90 g	plain chocolate, melted and cooled	3 oz
60 g	plain flour, sifted	2 oz
	cocoa powder to decorate	
	icing sugar to decorate	

Chestnut filling		
200 g	chestnut purée	7 oz
4 tbsp	single cream	4 tbsp
1 tbsp	thick honey	1 tbsp

Preheat the oven to 220°C (425°F or Mark 7). Place a small piece of non-stick parchment paper on a baking sheet. Grease a 32 by 22 cm (13 by 9 inch) Swiss roll tin and line it with parchment paper. If possible, have ready two piping bags fitted with 1.5 cm (½ inch) plain nozzles; one, however, will suffice.

Whisk the egg whites in a large bowl until they hold stiff peaks *(page 12)*, then whisk in 175 g (6 oz) of the caster sugar, 1 tablespoon at a time. To make a crisp meringue for the mushrooms adorning the log, transfer about 3 tablespoons of the mixture into a smaller bowl, ▶

and whisk in the remaining 15 g (½ oz) sugar. Spoon the smaller quantity of meringue into a piping bag and pipe mushroom stalks and caps on to the parchment paper as shown on page 86. Put the baking sheet on the bottom shelf of the oven.

Return any meringue left in the bag to the bulk of the mixture. Quickly fold in the melted chocolate and the flour with a metal spoon. Transfer this mixture to the second piping bag and pipe lines crosswise in the prepared tin, as shown on page 86. Bake the roulade for about 12 minutes, until risen and just firm to the touch. Take it out and switch the oven off, but leave the meringue mushrooms to cool slowly in the oven.

Turn the roulade out on to a sheet of parchment paper and peel off the lining paper. Loosely replace the lining paper over the cake, cover the cake with the tin and leave the cake to cool completely.

To make the filling, beat together the chestnut purée, cream and honey until smooth. Detach the cooled mushrooms from the paper and, using a dab of the chestnut filling, attach each stalk to a cap.

Remove the tin and lining paper from the cake and spread it with the filling. Roll up the log carefully, starting at one short end; use the parchment paper to help you. Put the log on a dish and arrange the mushrooms on and round it. Dust both log and mushrooms first with cocoa powder and then with icing sugar.

EDITOR'S NOTE: *To obtain 200 g (7 oz) of chestnut purée from fresh chestnuts, slit 400 g (14 oz) of chestnuts down one side, parboil them for 1 to 2 minutes, shell and peel them. Simmer the chestnuts in water for about 20 minutes, until they are tender. Drain and sieve them.*

Christmas Garland

THE SWEETNESS IN THIS CAKE COMES FROM ITS ABUNDANT FRUIT.
RICH AND MOIST WHEN FRESH, THIS CAKE WILL, HOWEVER, NOT KEEP
AS LONG AS A TRADITIONAL FRUIT CAKE BECAUSE OF THE LACK OF
BUTTER OR MARGARINE.

Serves 16
Working time: about 45 minutes
Total time: about 4 hours

Calories **270**
Protein **6g**
Cholesterol **50mg**
Fat **11g**
Saturated fat **2g**
Sodium **65mg**

1	orange, finely grated rind and juice	1
125 g	glacé cherries, chopped	4 oz
60 g	mixed candied peel, chopped	2 oz
30 g	angelica, chopped	1 oz
30 g	crystallized pineapple, chopped	1 oz
125 g	dried pears, chopped	4 oz
60 g	dried apricots, chopped	2 oz
60 g	sultanas	2 oz
60 g	currants	2 oz
60 g	raisins	2 oz
90 g	shelled walnuts, chopped	3 oz
90 g	shelled Brazil nuts, chopped	3 oz
60 g	shelled almonds, chopped	2 oz
125 g	wholemeal flour	4 oz
¼ tsp	ground cinnamon	¼ tsp
¼ tsp	ground allspice	¼ tsp
¼ tsp	ground cloves	¼ tsp
¼ tsp	grated nutmeg	¼ tsp
1 tsp	baking powder	1 tsp
3	eggs, beaten	3
1 tbsp	black treacle	1 tbsp
Icing and decoration		
125 g	icing sugar	4 oz
1 tbsp	brandy	1 tbsp
8	walnut halves	8
4	glacé cherries, quartered	4
	holly leaves for garnish	

Preheat the oven to 150°C (300°F or Mark 2). Grease a 20 cm (8 inch) ring mould.

Put the orange rind and juice in a large bowl. Stir in the chopped cherries, mixed peel, angelica, pineapple, pears, apricots, sultanas, currants, raisins, walnuts, Brazil nuts and almonds. Sift in the flour, cinnamon, allspice, cloves, nutmeg and baking powder, adding the bran left in the sieve. Pour in the eggs and treacle. Beat the mixture well with a wooden spoon. Transfer the mixture to the prepared mould and press it down.

Bake the cake for 45 minutes, or until it is firm to the touch. Leave it in the tin for 10 minutes, then invert it on to a wire tray and leave it to cool completely.

To make the icing, mix the icing sugar with the brandy and a little water, if necessary, to give a thin coating consistency. Spoon the icing over the cake, then decorate the cake with the walnut halves, cherry quarters and holly leaves.

Simnel Cake

A SIMNEL CAKE, TRADITIONALLY SERVED AT EASTERTIME, INCLUDES A CENTRAL LAYER OF MARZIPAN BAKED AS PART OF THE CAKE, AND 11 MARZIPAN BALLS ON TOP TO REPRESENT 11 OF JESUS' 12 APOSTLES; JUDAS, THE BETRAYER, IS OMITTED. IN THIS VERSION OF THE CAKE, THE MARZIPAN IS MADE WITH GROUND HAZELNUTS, WHICH CONTAIN LESS FAT THAN THE MORE COMMONLY USED GROUND ALMONDS.

Serves 16
Working time: about 50 minutes
Total time: about 7 hours and 30 minutes

Calories **325**
Protein **9g**
Cholesterol **40mg**
Total fat **4g**
Saturated fat **3g**
Sodium **75mg**

15 cl	skimmed milk	¼ pint
15 cl	fresh orange juice	¼ pint
60 g	unsalted butter	2 oz
175 g	dried apricots, chopped	6 oz
175 g	dried dates, chopped	6 oz
175 g	dried figs, chopped	6 oz
125 g	sultanas	4 oz
125 g	raisins	4 oz
60 g	currants	· 2 oz
125 g	soya flour	4 oz
½ tsp	ground cinnamon	½ tsp
¼ tsp	ground cloves	¼ tsp
¼ tsp	ground allspice	¼ tsp
1 tsp	grated nutmeg	1 tsp
175 g	wholemeal flour	6 oz
2	eggs, beaten	2
½ tsp	bicarbonate of soda	½ tsp
1 tsp	clear honey	1 tsp
2 tbsp	icing sugar	2 tbsp
Hazelnut marzipan		
125 g	shelled hazelnuts, ground	4 oz
90 g	wholemeal semolina	3 oz
125 g	light brown sugar	4 oz
½ tsp	almond extract	½ tsp
1	egg white	1

Preheat the oven to 140°C (275°F or Mark 1). Grease a deep 18 cm (7 inch) round cake tin. Double-line the tin with greaseproof paper and grease the paper. To protect the outside of the cake from scorching during the long cooking, tie a double thickness of brown paper round the outside of the tin and stand the tin on a baking sheet double-lined with brown paper.

Put the milk, orange juice and butter in a large saucepan. Bring the mixture to the boil. Add the apricots, dates, figs, sultanas, raisins and currants. Stir the fruit well and bring the liquid back to the boil, stirring occasionally. Remove the pan from the heat and leave the fruit to plump up, until it is barely warm.

Meanwhile, make the hazelnut marzipan. Mix the nuts, semolina, sugar and almond extract in a bowl. Add enough of the egg white to form a soft, pliable dough. Knead the marzipan on a lightly floured board until smooth. Cover the board with a large sheet of plastic film. On the plastic film, roll out one third of the marzipan and trim it to an 18 cm (7 inch) round. Set the remaining marzipan aside.

Sift the soya flour into a large bowl with the cinnamon, cloves, allspice and nutmeg. Add the wholemeal flour. When the fruit in the saucepan has cooled, add the eggs and bicarbonate of soda to the pan and stir well. Gradually stir the fruit into the flour mixture with a wooden spoon.

Spoon half of the cake batter into the prepared tin and level the top with a palette knife. Pick up the plastic film with the marzipan round on it and invert the marzipan on to the batter in the tin; spread the remaining cake batter over the marzipan and level the top with a small palette knife.

Bake the cake in the centre of the oven until risen and dark brown — 2 to 2½ hours. Test the cake by inserting a warm skewer into its centre. If the skewer is clean when removed, the cake is cooked; otherwise return the cake to the oven and test at 15-minute intervals. Leave the cake to cool in the tin, then turn it out and remove the lining paper.

From the unused marzipan make 11 balls about 2.5 cm (1 inch) in diameter. On the plastic film, roll the remaining marzipan into a round to fit the top of the cake. Brush the top of the cake with the honey and set the marzipan round in position. Flute the edge by pinching it with a thumb and forefinger. Arrange the 11 marzipan balls round the edge of the cake, attaching them with a dab of the honey.

Place the cake on a grill rack. Set it on the grill floor under a moderate grill. To flavour the marzipan and cook the semolina in it, leave the cake under the grill until the marzipan is lightly browned — about 10 minutes. Let the marzipan cool.

Sift the icing sugar into a bowl. Mix in 2 teaspoons of water and beat until the icing is smooth. Pour the icing over the centre of the cake and leave it to set.

EDITOR'S NOTE: *For a light-coloured marzipan, use yellow semolina and caster sugar in place of the wholemeal semolina and brown sugar. Three oranges should yield 15 to 20 cl (5 to 7 fl oz) of juice.*

Golden Passion Pavlova

A CONFECTION OF MERINGUE AND FRUIT, PAVLOVA WAS CREATED IN 1935 BY AN AUSTRALIAN CHEF AND NAMED IN HONOUR OF THE GREAT RUSSIAN BALLERINA, WHO HAD RECENTLY TOURED THE ANTIPODES. HERE, THE TRADITIONAL WHIPPED CREAM FILLING IS REPLACED BY A MIXTURE OF CREAM, CURD CHEESE AND YOGURT.

Serves 10
Working time: about 25 minutes
Total time: about 2 hours and 40 minutes

Calories **90**
Protein **3g**
Cholesterol **25mg**
Total fat **3g**
Saturated fat **2g**
Sodium **95mg**

2 tsp	cornflour	2 tsp
1 tsp	vinegar	1 tsp
½ tsp	pure vanilla extract	½ tsp
3	egg whites	3
⅛ tsp	cream of tartar	⅛ tsp
125 g	demerara sugar	4 oz
2	kiwi fruits, peeled and sliced	2
1	mango, peeled and chopped	1
Passion cream filling		
175 g	medium-fat curd cheese	6 oz
4 tbsp	double cream	4 tbsp
2 tbsp	plain low-fat yogurt	2 tbsp
2 tsp	clear honey	2 tsp
2	passion fruits	2

Preheat the oven to 140°C (275°F or Mark 1). Line a baking sheet with non-stick parchment paper. Draw a 20 cm (8 inch) circle on the paper in pencil, then turn the paper over.

Blend together the cornflour, vinegar and vanilla extract in a small bowl. Whisk the egg whites and cream of tartar in a large bowl until the whites stand in stiff peaks *(page 12)*. Add a quarter of the sugar at a time to the whites, whisking well after each addition. Spoon in the cornflour blend and whisk until the meringue is glossy and thick enough to hold soft peaks.

Transfer the meringue to a large piping bag fitted with a medium star nozzle. Pipe a series of swirls round the outside of the marked circle on the paper. Pipe two thirds of the remaining meringue within the circle. Smooth the meringue with a palette knife and make sure there are no gaps. With the remaining meringue, pipe a second series of swirls on top of the first ones to create a raised border.

Bake the Pavlova in the centre of the oven for 1 hour. Turn off the heat, open the oven door a fraction and leave the Pavlova to cool slowly. It will take about another hour.

To make the passion cream filling, mix the curd cheese, cream, yogurt and honey in a bowl with a wooden spoon, then beat them until smooth. Put 2 tablespoons of the filling into a nylon piping bag fitted with a medium star nozzle. Halve the passion fruits. Scoop out the flesh of the fruit with a teaspoon and stir it into the remaining filling.

Carefully peel the paper away from the meringue and place the meringue on a flat plate. With the filling in the piping bag, pipe a circle of swirls just inside the raised meringue border. Spread the passion cream filling inside the cream swirls. Cover the filling with the kiwi fruit slices and chopped mango.

EDITOR'S NOTE: *The meringue for the Pavlova can be cooked in advance and stored for up to a week in an airtight container.*

Hazelnut and Raspberry Galette

Serves 12
Working time: about 1 hour
Total time: about 2 hours

Calories **165**
Protein **5g**
Cholesterol **65mg**
Total fat **8g**
Saturated fat **3g**
Sodium **70mg**

3	eggs	3
30 g	caster sugar	1 oz
30 g	wholemeal flour	1 oz
½ tsp	pure vanilla extract	½ tsp
250 g	thick Greek yogurt	8 oz
300 g	fresh raspberries, or frozen raspberries, thawed	10 oz
4 tbsp	double cream, whipped	4 tbsp
Hazelnut meringue		
3	egg whites	3
⅛ tsp	salt	⅛ tsp
90 g	caster sugar	3 oz
90 g	shelled hazelnuts, toasted, skinned and finely chopped	3 oz
1 tbsp	cornflour	1 tbsp

Preheat the oven to 200°C (400°F or Mark 6). Grease two 32 by 22 cm (13 by 9 inch) Swiss roll tins. Line them with non-stick parchment paper and lightly grease the paper.

To make the hazelnut meringue, whisk the egg whites with the salt until the mixture stands in stiff peaks *(page 12)*, then gradually whisk in the sugar 1 tablespoon at a time, whisking well between each addition. Mix the hazelnuts with the cornflour and fold them into the meringue. Spread the meringue evenly in one of the prepared tins and bake it for 20 minutes. Leave it to get cold in the tin. Reduce the oven to 180°C (350°F or Mark 4).

Whisk the eggs and sugar in a bowl over a pan of simmering water until pale and thick *(page 12)*. Remove from the heat and whisk until cool. Fold in the flour and vanilla, then transfer to the second tin and level the surface. Bake the sponge for about 15 minutes, until just firm to the touch. Leave it to cool.

Remove the sponge and the meringue from their tins. Trim them to the same size. Cut each of them in half lengthwise. Crumble the meringue trimmings and stir them into the yogurt. Spread the yogurt over one layer of meringue and both layers of sponge.

Reserve 30 raspberries, then divide the remainder among the three layers spread with yogurt. Place a sponge layer on a serving dish. Cover it with the decorated meringue layer, then the second sponge layer and finally the remaining meringue layer. Press the top layer down gently. Using a piping bag fitted with a medium star nozzle, pipe lines of cream across the top. Arrange the raspberries between the cream.

EDITOR'S NOTE: *To toast and skin hazelnuts, place them on a baking sheet in a 180°C (350°F or Mark 4) oven for 10 minutes. Enfold them in a towel and rub briskly to loosen the skins. The galette can be made with strawberries instead of raspberries; redcurrants can be mixed with either alternative.*

Meringue Coffee Torte

Serves 12
Working time: about 50 minutes
Total time: about 2 hours and 30 minutes

Calories **165**
Protein **10g**
Cholesterol **45mg**
Total fat **6g**
Saturated fat **1g**
Sodium **220mg**

30 g	light brown sugar	1 oz
2	eggs	2
60 g	brown flour	2 oz
½ tsp	baking powder	½ tsp
300 g	skimmed-milk soft cheese	10 oz
4 tbsp	double cream	4 tbsp
1 tbsp	clear honey	1 tbsp
3 tsp	strong black coffee	3 tsp
	icing sugar to decorate	
18	walnut halves	18
	Walnut meringue	
2	egg whites	2
90 g	demerara sugar	3 oz
45 g	shelled walnuts, finely chopped	1½ oz
2 tsp	cornflour	2 tsp

Preheat the oven to 180°C (350°F or Mark 4). Grease a 20 cm (8 inch) round cake tin. Line its base with greaseproof paper and grease the paper.

Put the brown sugar and eggs in a bowl set over simmering water. Whisk the mixture by hand or with an electric whisk until thick and pale (page 12). Remove the bowl from the heat and whisk until the whisk, when lifted, leaves a trail on the surface. Sift the flour and baking powder together into the mixture. Using a spatula or large metal or plastic spoon, fold in the flour. Pour the mixture into the prepared tin and level the top with a small palette knife.

Bake the sponge in the centre of the oven until risen, lightly coloured and springy when touched in the centre — 15 to 20 minutes. Leave the cake in the tin for 5 minutes, then turn it out on to a wire rack. Remove the paper and leave the cake to cool.

To make the walnut meringue, reduce the oven setting to 130°C (250°F or Mark ½). Line a baking sheet with non-stick parchment paper. Draw two 18.5 cm (7½ inch) circles on the parchment and invert the parchment. (The meringue circles are smaller than the tin in which the sponge rounds cook because meringue, unlike sponge, does not shrink as it cools.) In a large bowl, whisk the egg whites until they hold stiff peaks (page 12). Add one third of the sugar at a time, whisking well after each addition. Mix together the walnuts and cornflour, and fold them into the meringue.

Divide the walnut meringue between the two circles and spread it evenly. Bake the rounds for 1 hour to 1 hour and 20 minutes, until the meringue feels firm and no longer sticky. Transfer the parchment with the meringue rounds to a wire rack. When the meringue is cold, peel off the parchment.

Beat the cheese and cream in a bowl with a wooden spoon. Stir in the honey and coffee. Put 2 tablespoons of the coffee cream in a piping bag fitted with a medium star nozzle.

Place a meringue round on a plate and spread it with one third of the remaining coffee cream. Slice the sponge in half horizontally. Set one layer on the meringue and spread it with another third of the coffee cream. Top the coffee cream with the remaining layer of sponge, the rest of the coffee cream, and finally the second meringue round.

Dust the torte with the icing sugar. Pipe coffee cream scrolls round the top edge of the torte and decorate it with the walnut halves.

3 A sprinkling of caster sugar provides the finishing touch for madeleines — scallop-shaped mouthfuls of golden sponge.

Small-Scale Delights

Cooked rapidly and cooled in minutes instead of hours, small cakes provide all the pleasures of home baking without deferment. Miniature form does not limit the cook's scope: the range of recipes in this chapter reflects both the plain cakes of Chapter 1 and the gateaux of Chapter 2.

Perhaps the simplest small cakes to make are the tray bakes, where a mixture is spread out in a shallow tin and sliced into individual squares, bars or triangles after baking. (Instructions for lining tins appear on page 13.) Many of the tray-bake recipes here are for robust mixtures of whole grain, dried fruit and nuts.

The small cakes that are individually shaped before baking take the shortest time of all to cook. Some of those presented on pages 104 to 116 are formed into rounds or crescents by hand, others stamped with a cutter into shapes that cook individually on a baking sheet, yet others poured into trays with individual depressions. Fluted and ridged moulds, such as the madeleine tin pictured on the left, impress their contours on the mouthfuls that bake in them with very decorative results.

Most of the assemblages on pages 116 to 125 start out like tray bakes, with a cake mixture baked as a sheet in a shallow tin. But the character of the assemblages is very different, for they are based not on wholefood ingredients but on a feather-light, low-fat sponge. Instead of being simply sliced after cooking, the sponge is sometimes split horizontally and sandwiched together with fruit purée or lemon curd; it may be shaped with cutters into rounds, ovals or stars and coated with cream, nuts, chocolate or marzipan. The result is a collection of exquisite morsels, well repaying the minutes devoted to their construction. The superfluous sponge left after stamping out shapes makes a good basis for a trifle.

Date and Apricot Triangles

HAZELNUT PASTE CONTAINS LESS FAT AND FEWER CALORIES THAN
THE MORE COMMONLY MADE ALMOND PASTE. THE GROUND RICE IN
THIS RECIPE EXTENDS THE MIXTURE WITHOUT INCREASING THE FAT
CONTENT, AND CONTRIBUTES A PLEASANTLY CRUNCHY TEXTURE.

Serves 24
Working time: about 40 minutes
Total time: about 2 hours and 40 minutes

Calories **200**
Protein **3g**
Cholesterol **30mg**
Total fat **8g**
Saturated fat **2g**
Sodium **60mg**

250 g	dried apricots, chopped	8 oz
250 g	dried dates, chopped	8 oz
125 g	raisins	4 oz
3 tbsp	malt extract	3 tbsp
125 g	polyunsaturated margarine	4 oz
125 g	dark brown sugar	4 oz
3	large eggs	3
200 g	wholemeal flour	7 oz
1 tsp	ground cinnamon	1 tsp
½ tsp	ground nutmeg	½ tsp
1 tbsp	apricot jam without added sugar	1 tbsp
Hazelnut paste		
150 g	hazelnuts, skinned and ground	5 oz
150 g	caster sugar	5 oz
60 g	ground rice	2 oz
1	large egg white	1
2 tsp	rose water	2 tsp

Preheat the oven to 170°C (325°F or Mark 3). Grease
a 28 by 18 cm (11 by 7 inch) baking tin. Line it with
greaseproof paper and grease the paper. Cover the
apricots with boiling water; leave them to soak for 30
minutes and then drain them.

Put the apricots, dates and raisins in a bowl and stir
in the malt extract. In another bowl, beat the margarine
and brown sugar with a wooden spoon until they are
fluffy, then beat in the eggs one at a time, adding a
little flour with each egg. Mix in the remaining flour, the
cinnamon, nutmeg and the fruits.

Turn the batter into the baking tin and smooth it to
the tin's edges. Bake the cake for 30 minutes, then
reduce the heat to 150°C (300°F or Mark 2) and cook
for a further 40 minutes until the mixture is firm in the
centre. Loosen the cake from the tin and turn it on to a
wire rack to cool. Remove the lining paper.

For the hazelnut paste, mix the hazelnuts, caster
sugar and ground rice together. Make a well in the
centre and stir in the egg white and rose water until the
mixture binds together.

Heat the jam with ½ tablespoon of water, then sieve
the diluted jam. Brush it over the base of the cake
while the glaze is still warm. Roll the hazelnut paste
out to a rectangle the same size as the cake, using
ground rice to prevent it from sticking to the board.

Drape the paste rectangle over the rolling pin and transfer it to the cake. Neaten the edges, then score the top of the paste with a sharp knife to make a lattice pattern. Put the cake under a hot grill for 1 to 2 minutes, until the hazelnut paste is tinged with brown. Cut the cake into triangles to serve.

EDITOR'S NOTE: *To skin hazelnuts, first loosen their skins by roasting them on a baking sheet in a 180°C (350°F or Mark 4) oven for 10 minutes. Tip the nuts on to a towel and rub them to loosen the skins. Grind the nuts in a rotary grinder or a food processor; a rotary grinder is preferable because it gives a uniform texture without drawing the oil out of the nuts.*

Honey Squares

Serves 24
Working time: about 30 minutes
Total time: about 1 hour and 40 minutes

Calories **160**
Protein **3g**
Cholesterol **5mg**
Total fat **8g**
Saturated fat **1g**
Sodium **85mg**

250 g	plain flour	8 oz
3 tsp	baking powder	3 tsp
125 g	wholemeal flour	4 oz
2	lemons, finely grated rind only	2
190 g	clear honey	6½ oz
60 g	unsalted butter	2 oz
6 tbsp	safflower oil	6 tbsp
60 g	dark muscovado sugar	2 oz
1	egg	1
1	egg white	1
6 tbsp	buttermilk	6 tbsp
6 tbsp	skimmed milk	6 tbsp
30 g	blanched almonds, split and lightly toasted	1 oz
6	glacé cherries, quartered	6
15 g	angelica, cut into leaf shapes	½ oz

Preheat the oven to 180°C (350°F or Mark 4). Grease a rectangular 30 by 20 by 3 cm (12 by 8 by 1¼ inch) baking tin and line it with non-stick parchment paper.

Sift the plain flour and baking powder into a bowl; mix in the wholemeal flour and lemon rind and make a well in the centre.

Reserving 1 tablespoon of honey, put the remainder into a saucepan with the butter, oil and sugar. Heat gently until the butter is melted. Let the mixture cool slightly. Very lightly whisk the egg and the egg white together, then whisk in the buttermilk and milk. Pour the honey and egg mixtures into the centre of the flour. Stir well, then pour the batter into the prepared tin, spreading it evenly.

Bake the honey cake for 35 to 40 minutes, until well risen, firm and springy to the touch. Remove it from the oven and immediately brush the top with the reserved tablespoonful of honey. Arrange the almonds, glacé cherries and angelica leaves on the cake. Cut the cake into squares when it has cooled.

Coconut Bars

Serves 20
Working time: about 25 minutes
Total time: about 1 hour and 45 minutes

Calories **100**
Protein **2g**
Cholesterol **36mg**
Total fat **4g**
Saturated fat **3g**
Sodium **18mg**

3	eggs, separated	3
125 g	caster sugar	4 oz
½	lemon, grated rind and juice	½
60 g	semolina	2 oz
30 g	ground almonds	1 oz
Chewy coconut topping		
2	egg whites	2
90 g	demerara sugar	3 oz
90 g	desiccated coconut	3 oz

Preheat the oven to 180°C (350°F or Mark 4). Grease a 28 by 18 cm (11 by 7 inch) baking tin, line its base with greaseproof paper and grease the paper.

Cream the egg yolks with the sugar, lemon rind and juice until the mixture is thick. Stir in the semolina and ground almonds. Whisk the egg whites until they are stiff, then fold them into the creamed mixture. Turn the batter into the baking tin and level the batter's surface.

To make the topping, whisk the two egg whites until they are stiff, then fold in the demerara sugar and coconut. Lay dessertspoons of the topping at regular intervals on top of the cake batter. (Larger spoonfuls would sink down into the light sponge mixture.) With a fork, carefully tease the topping into an even layer that reaches to the tin's edge.

Bake the coconut cake for 35 to 40 minutes, until golden. Turn the cake out on to a rack; the coconut topping will be quite firm, and will not crumble. Remove the lining paper, then reverse the cake again on to a second rack. When the cake is cool, cut it into bars with a sharp, serrated knife.

Fig Bars

Serves 18
Working time: about 25 minutes
Total time: about 2 hours

Calories **145**
Protein **3g**
Cholesterol **0mg**
Total fat **9g**
Saturated fat **2g**
Sodium **85mg**

300 g	dried figs, finely chopped	10 oz
5 tbsp	apple juice	5 tbsp
150 g	wholemeal flour	5 oz
150 g	polyunsaturated margarine	5 oz
150 g	rolled oats	5 oz
45 g	muscovado sugar	1½ oz
2 tbsp	sesame seeds, browned	2 tbsp

Preheat the oven to 190°C (375°F or Mark 5). Grease and line a 20 cm (8 inch) square shallow baking tin.

Put the figs in a saucepan with the apple juice and simmer for 5 minutes, stirring occasionally, until the figs are soft. Set the pan aside. Put the flour and margarine in a bowl and blend them together with a fork. Add the oats, sugar and sesame seeds and rub the mixture until it resembles coarse breadcrumbs.

Press half of the oat mixture into the tin. Spread the figs and apple juice on top, then sprinkle over the remaining oat mixture. Press the top oat layer down firmly with a palette knife. Bake the fig cake for 40 to 50 minutes, until its top is golden.

Cut the cake into bars while warm, but leave them in the tin to cool completely.

SUGGESTED ACCOMPANIMENT: *chilled apple juice.*

EDITOR'S NOTE: *To brown sesame seeds, sprinkle a layer of seeds in a heavy-based pan, cover and cook over high heat. When they begin to pop, keep the pan on the heat for 1 minute more but shake it constantly.*

Apple Streusel Slices

Serves 20
Working time: about 40 minutes
Total time: about 2 hours

Calories **135**
Protein **2g**
Cholesterol **0mg**
Total fat **5g**
Saturated fat **1g**
Sodium **55mg**

100 g	polyunsaturated margarine	3½ oz
200 g	wholemeal flour	7 oz
750 g	dessert apples, peeled, cored and chopped	1½ lb
60 g	dark brown sugar	2 oz
2 tsp	ground cinnamon	2 tsp
90 g	sultanas	3 oz
Sesame streusel		
30 g	polyunsaturated margarine	1 oz
75 g	wholemeal flour	2½ oz
30 g	demerara sugar	1 oz
1½ tbsp	sesame seeds	1½ tbsp
1 tsp	ground cinnamon	1 tsp

Rub the margarine into the flour in a bowl until the mixture resembles breadcrumbs. Stir in about 3 tablespoons of iced water — enough to make a fairly firm dough — and knead lightly until the dough is smooth. Wrap the dough in plastic film and leave it to rest for 10 minutes.

Roll the dough out thinly on a lightly floured surface, and use it to line a 30 by 20 cm (12 by 8 inch) Swiss roll tin. Prick the dough with a fork and refrigerate it for about 15 minutes.

Meanwhile, preheat the oven to 200°C (400°F or Mark 6). Put the chopped apples in a bowl, with the sugar, cinnamon and sultanas, and mix them together.

To make the sesame streusel, rub the margarine into the flour in a bowl until the mixture resembles breadcrumbs. Stir in the sugar, sesame seeds and cinnamon. Sprinkle 3 tablespoons of the mixture over the dough in the tin to absorb the juice from the apples. Spread the apple mixture in the tin. Sprinkle the remaining streusel over the apples. Bake the cake for 30 to 35 minutes, until the streusel is golden-brown. Cut the cake into slices when it has cooled.

Lemon Semolina Squares

Serves 15
Working time: about 30 minutes
Total time: about 2 hours

Calories **150**
Protein **3g**
Cholesterol **30mg**
Total fat **7g**
Saturated fat **2g**
Sodium **100mg**

90 g	polyunsaturated margarine	3 oz
125 g	caster sugar	4 oz
1	lemon, grated rind and juice	1
150 g	wholemeal flour	5 oz
2 tsp	baking powder	2 tsp
2	large eggs	2
90 g	semolina	3 oz
30 g	ground almonds	1 oz
15 cl	plain low-fat yogurt	¼ pint
15 g	pine-nuts	½ oz
4 tbsp	clear honey	4 tbsp

Preheat the oven to 180°C (350°F or Mark 4). Grease a 28 by 18 cm (11 by 7 inch) baking tin.

Cream the margarine and sugar together with the lemon rind until the mixture is light and fluffy. Sift the flour with the baking powder, adding the bran left in the sieve. Beat the eggs one at a time into the creamed margarine and sugar, adding 1 tablespoon of the flour mixture with the second egg. Fold in the remaining flour and baking powder, together with the semolina, almonds and yogurt.

Turn the batter into the baking tin and spread the mixture evenly to the edges. Sprinkle over the pine-nuts and press them gently into the batter. Bake the sponge for 40 minutes, or until the cake springs back when pressed in the centre.

Make a syrup by heating the honey with 15 cl (¼ pint) of water in a small pan. Boil the syrup for 1 minute, then stir in the lemon juice.

When the sponge is cooked, prick it all over with a fork and slowly pour over the warm syrup. Leave the sponge to absorb the syrup. When cool, cut the cake into squares and remove them from the tin.

Almond-Apricot Fingers

Serves 18
Working time: about 30 minutes
Total time: about 2 hours

Calories **150**
Protein **3g**
Cholesterol **25mg**
Total fat **9g**
Saturated fat **2g**
Sodium **100mg**

125 g	wholemeal flour	4 oz
2 tsp	baking powder	2 tsp
125 g	polyunsaturated margarine	4 oz
90 g	light muscovado sugar	3 oz
2	eggs	2
175 g	dried apricots, chopped and soaked for 30 minutes in boiling water	6 oz
60 g	ground almonds	2 oz
½ tsp	almond extract	½ tsp
30 g	flaked almonds	1 oz

Preheat the oven to 190°C (375°F or Mark 5). Line the base of a 30 by 20 cm (12 by 8 inch) baking tin with greaseproof paper and grease the paper.

Sift the wholemeal flour with the baking powder, adding the bran left in the sieve. Cream the margarine and sugar together in a bowl until fluffy. Beat in the eggs one at a time, adding 1 tablespoon of the flour mixture with each egg.

Drain the apricots thoroughly, reserving 1 table-spoon of the soaking liquid. Stir the apricots into the batter and fold in the remaining flour mixture, together with the ground almonds, almond extract and reserved apricot soaking liquid. Turn the mixture into the baking tin. Spread it evenly to the edges and sprinkle the flaked almonds over the top.

Bake the cake for 30 to 35 minutes, until it springs back when pressed in the centre. Turn the cake out on to a wire rack, remove the lining paper, then reverse the cake on to another rack to cool. Cut the cake into fingers when it has cooled.

Hazelnut-Pineapple Slices

Serves 12
Working time: about 30 minutes
Total time: about 3 hours and 30 minutes

Calories **185**
Protein **4g**
Cholesterol **0mg**
Total fat **6g**
Saturated fat **1g**
Sodium **15mg**

175 g	plain flour	6 oz
⅛ tsp	salt	⅛ tsp
30 g	light brown sugar	1 oz
½ tsp	ground cinnamon	½ tsp
1	orange, finely grated rind only	1
30 g	unsalted butter	1 oz
15 g	fresh yeast, or 7 g (¼ oz) dried yeast	½ oz
6 tbsp	skimmed milk, tepid	6 tbsp
2 tbsp	apricot jam without added sugar	2 tbsp
30 g	shelled hazelnuts, thinly sliced	1 oz
Hazelnut-pineapple layer		
2	pineapples	2
100 g	shelled hazelnuts, toasted, skinned and finely ground	3½ oz
60 g	demerara sugar	2 oz

Sift the flour, salt, sugar and cinnamon into a bowl. Mix in the orange rind, then rub in the butter until the mixture resembles fine breadcrumbs. Dissolve the yeast in the milk; if using dried yeast, leave it to stand, following the manufacturer's instructions. Pour the yeast liquid into the flour and mix to form a soft dough. Knead the dough on a lightly floured surface for 2 to 3 minutes to smooth it. Put it in a clean bowl. Cover the bowl with plastic film and leave it in a warm place for about 1 hour, until the dough has doubled in size.

Meanwhile, remove the skin and eyes from the pineapples. Cut the flesh into slices about 5 mm (¼ inch) thick. Remove the core from each slice with a small plain cutter. Trim the slices into neat rounds, using a large metal cutter as a guide. Put the pineapple rings aside until needed.

Re-knead the risen dough for 1 minute, then roll it out into an oblong large enough to fit a 32 by 22 by 2 cm (13 by 9 by ¾ inch) baking tray. Butter the tray, then place the dough in the tray, pressing it out to fit exactly. Prick the dough well all over. Cover the tray with plastic film and leave it in a warm place for 30 to 40 minutes, until the dough has risen slightly. Meanwhile, preheat the oven to 200°C (400°F or Mark 6).

Sprinkle the ground hazelnuts evenly all over the risen dough. Neatly arrange the pineapple rings, overlapping, in rows on top. Sprinkle the demerara sugar evenly over the pineapple. Leave the assembly to stand for 5 minutes so the sugar has time to dissolve, then bake for 30 to 35 minutes, until the pineapple rings have softened and are very lightly browned.

Heat the apricot jam in a small pan until it boils. Sieve it and brush it evenly over the hot pineapple rings. Sprinkle the pineapple with sliced hazelnuts. Leave the cake to cool before slicing it.

EDITOR'S NOTE: *To toast and skin hazelnuts, place them in a preheated 180°C (350°F or Mark 4) oven for 10 minutes. Enfold them in a towel and rub briskly to loosen the skins.*

Apricot Tray Bake

Serves 16
Working time: about 45 minutes
Total time: about 3 hours

Calories **200**
Protein **7g**
Cholesterol **25mg**
Total fat **11g**
Saturated fat **4g**
Sodium **75mg**

250 g	medium-fat curd cheese	8 oz
45 g	caster sugar	1½ oz
1	egg, beaten	1
125 g	ground almonds	4 oz
1	lemon, finely grated rind only	1
16	large apricots	16
15 g	icing sugar	½ oz
1 tbsp	apricot jam without added sugar	1 tbsp
15 g	pistachio nuts, skinned and very finely sliced	½ oz

Yeast dough

175 g	plain flour	6 oz
30 g	vanilla sugar	1 oz
1	lemon, finely grated rind only	1
60 g	unsalted butter	2 oz
15 g	fresh yeast or 7 g (¼ oz) dried yeast	½ oz
6 tbsp	skimmed milk, tepid	6 tbsp

To make the yeast dough, sift the flour into a bowl, mix in the vanilla-flavoured sugar and lemon rind, then rub in the butter until the mixture resembles fine bread-crumbs. Dissolve the yeast in the tepid milk; if using dried yeast, leave it to stand, following the manufac-turer's instructions. Pour the yeast liquid into the flour and mix to form a soft dough. On a very lightly floured surface, knead the dough for 2 to 3 minutes to smooth

it. Put the dough in a clean bowl. Cover the bowl with plastic film and leave it in a warm place for about 1 hour, or until the dough has doubled in size.

Knead the risen dough for 1 minute, then roll it out to form an oblong large enough to fit a 32 by 22 by 2 cm (13 by 9 by ¾ inch) baking tray. Butter the tray. Lower the dough into the tray, pressing it out to fit exactly. Prick the dough all over with a fork. Cover the tray with plastic film and leave it in a warm place for 30 to 40 minutes, until the dough has risen slightly.

Meanwhile, heat the oven to 200°C (400°F or Mark 6). Put the curd cheese in a bowl with the caster sugar, egg, almonds and lemon rind. With a wooden spoon, beat them together until smooth. Spread the cheese mixture evenly over the risen dough.

Drop the apricots into simmering water for 10 to 15 seconds to loosen their skins. Remove the apricots, skin them, halve them and stone them. Arrange the apricot halves on top of the cheese mixture, spacing them evenly. Sift the icing sugar over the apricots. Leave the cake to stand for 2 minutes to allow the sugar to dissolve, then bake the cake for 30 to 35 minutes, until the cheese mixture is set and lightly browned and the apricots are soft.

Heat the apricot jam in a small pan until it is boiling hot, and brush it over the apricots. Sprinkle them with the pistachio nuts. Allow the tray bake to cool in the tin. Slice it when it has cooled completely.

EDITOR'S NOTE: *To skin pistachio nuts, drop them into boiling water and simmer them for 1 minute. Drain them, enfold them in a towel and rub them briskly.*

Coffee Butterfly Cakes

Makes 12 cakes
Working time: about 35 minutes
Total time: about 1 hour and 30 minutes

Per cake:
Calories **180**
Protein **2g**
Cholesterol **20mg**
Total fat **9g**
Saturated fat **5g**
Sodium **45mg**

125 g	unsalted butter	4 oz
60 g	light brown sugar	2 oz
60 g	clear honey	2 oz
2 tbsp	strong black coffee	2 tbsp
2	egg whites, lightly beaten	2
175 g	plain flour	6 oz
1½ tsp	baking powder	1½ tsp
15 cl	rum-flavoured pastry cream (page 16)	¼ pint
1 tsp	icing sugar	1 tsp

Preheat the oven to 180°C (350°F or Mark 4). Butter 12 deep, sloping-sided bun tins. Dust the tins lightly with a little flour.

Use a wooden spoon or electric mixer to beat the butter in a bowl with the brown sugar and honey until soft. Add the black coffee and 1 tablespoon of warm water, and continue beating until the mixture becomes very light and fluffy. Gradually beat in the egg whites. Sift the flour and baking powder together over the creamed mixture, then fold them in carefully with a metal spoon or rubber spatula.

Divide the mixture evenly among the prepared tins. Bake the cakes for 15 to 20 minutes, until well risen, springy to the touch and very slightly shrunk from the sides of the tins. Leave the cakes in the tins for 2 to 3 minutes, then transfer them to a wire rack to cool.

Using a small, sharp, pointed knife held at an angle, carefully cut a cone out of the centre of each cake. Cut each cone in half.

Put the rum-flavoured pastry cream in a piping bag fitted with a medium-sized star nozzle. Pipe a whirl of pastry cream into the middle of each cake. Then replace the two halves of each cone on top of the cream, angling them to mimic butterfly wings. Sift the icing sugar lightly over the cakes.

Cherry and Walnut Buns

Makes 24 buns
Working time: about 25 minutes
Total time: about 2 hours and 45 minutes

Per bun:
Calories **140**
Protein **3g**
Cholesterol **20mg**
Total fat **6g**
Saturated fat **3g**
Sodium **15mg**

60 g	glacé cherries, chopped	2 oz
125 g	dried dates, stoned and chopped	4 oz
2 tbsp	rum	2 tbsp
250 g	plain flour	8 oz
⅛ tsp	salt	⅛ tsp
125 g	wholemeal flour	4 oz
60 g	light brown sugar	2 oz
60 g	unsalted butter	2 oz
1	lemon, finely grated rind only	1
15 g	fresh yeast or 7g (¼ oz) dried yeast	½ oz
¼ litre	skimmed milk, tepid	8 fl oz
1	egg	1
4 tbsp	safflower oil	4 tbsp
60 g	shelled walnuts, chopped	2 oz
1 tsp	icing sugar	1 tsp

Put the cherries and dates into a small bowl with the rum and mix well. Cover the fruit and set it aside.

Sift the plain flour and salt into a large bowl. Mix in the wholemeal flour and brown sugar. Rub the butter into the flours until the mixture resembles fine bread-crumbs. Mix in the lemon rind. Dissolve the yeast in the milk; if using dried yeast, leave it to stand, following, the manufacturer's instructions. Whisk the egg and oil together. Pour the yeast liquid and egg mixture into the flours and beat the dough with a wooden spoon or electric beater until smooth and elasticated — about 5 minutes. Cover the bowl with plastic film and leave the dough in a warm place for about 1 hour until doubled in size. Meanwhile, butter and lightly flour two 12-hole deep bun tin trays.

Beat the dates and cherries, and 30 g (1 oz) of the walnuts into the risen dough. Divide the dough evenly among the prepared bun tins. Cover loosely with plastic film and leave in a warm place until the dough rises to the top of the tins — 30 to 40 minutes. Meanwhile, preheat the oven to 200°C (400°F or Mark 6).

When the dough has risen to the top of the tins, sprinkle the remaining walnuts on top of the buns and bake them for 20 to 25 minutes, until well risen, golden-brown and slightly shrunk from the sides of the tins. Turn the buns on to wire racks. When they have cooled, sift the icing sugar over the buns.

Banana and Cardamom Cakes

Makes 18 cakes
Working time: about 20 minutes
Total time: about 50 minutes

Per cake:
Calories **145**
Protein **3g**
Cholesterol **25mg**
Total fat **9g**
Saturated fat **2g**
Sodium **115mg**

125 g	polyunsaturated margarine	4 oz
90 g	brown sugar	3 oz
10	cardamom pods, seeds only, finely chopped	10
125 g	wholemeal flour	4 oz
2 tsp	baking powder	2 tsp
2	eggs	2
2	medium bananas, mashed	2
60 g	ground almonds	2 oz
Creamy topping		
90 g	medium-fat curd cheese	3 oz
2 tsp	clear honey	2 tsp
1 tbsp	plain low-fat yogurt	1 tbsp

Preheat the oven to 190°C (375°F or Mark 5). Grease and flour 18 bun tins.

In a bowl, cream the margarine and sugar together with the cardamom seeds until the mixture is fluffy. Sift the flour with the baking powder, adding the bran left in the sieve. With a wooden spoon, beat the eggs into the margarine and sugar one at a time, adding a tablespoon of the flour with each egg. Beat in the bananas and almonds, then fold in the remaining flour.

Divide the batter among the bun tins and bake the cakes for 15 minutes, until the centres spring back when pressed. Loosen the cakes from the tins with a small knife and put them on a wire rack to cool.

To make the topping, beat the curd cheese with the honey and yogurt. When the blend is smooth, spoon it into a piping bag fitted with a medium-sized star nozzle and pipe a rosette on each cake.

Cinnamon Rock Cakes

MOST ROCK CAKE RECIPES CALL FOR ABOUT HALF AS MUCH FAT AS FLOUR; THIS RECIPE CUTS DOWN ON THE BUTTER, AND SUBSTITUTES YOGURT AND SKIMMED MILK FOR MOISTURE. BECAUSE OF THEIR LOW FAT CONTENT, THESE CAKES DO NOT KEEP WELL AND SHOULD BE EATEN THE DAY THEY ARE BAKED.

Makes 16 cakes
Working time: about 20 minutes
Total time: about 1 hour

Per cake:
Calories **135**
Protein **3g**
Cholesterol **25mg**
Total fat **4g**
Saturated fat **2g**
Sodium **90mg**

125 g	plain flour	4 oz
2 tsp	baking powder	2 tsp
½ tsp	grated nutmeg	½ tsp
1 tsp	ground cinnamon	1 tsp
125 g	wholemeal flour	4 oz
60 g	dark brown sugar	2 oz
1	lemon, finely grated rind only	1
60 g	unsalted butter	2 oz
90 g	raisins	3 oz
90 g	sultanas	3 oz
1	egg, beaten	1
2 tbsp	plain low-fat yogurt	2 tbsp
6 tbsp	skimmed milk	6 tbsp
2 tsp	caster sugar	2 tsp

Preheat the oven to 220°C (425°F or Mark 7). Butter and lightly flour two baking sheets.

Sift the plain flour, baking powder, nutmeg and half of the cinnamon into a bowl. Mix in the wholemeal flour, brown sugar and lemon rind. Rub the butter into the flours until the mixture resembles fine breadcrumbs. Mix in the raisins and sultanas, then make a well into the centre. Put the egg, yogurt and milk into the well and stir to form a fairly soft mixture.

Space heaped teaspoons of the mixture well apart on the prepared baking sheets. Bake for 15 to 20 minutes until the rock cakes are well risen, golden-brown and firm to the touch. Transfer the rock cakes from the baking trays to wire racks to cool.

Mix the caster sugar with the remaining cinnamon and sprinkle the combination over the rock cakes.

Loganberry Surprise Buns

Makes 15 buns
Working time: about 20 minutes
Total time: about 1 hour

Per bun:
Calories **145**
Protein **2g**
Cholesterol **15mg**
Total fat **8g**
Saturated fat **5g**
Sodium **35mg**

125 g	unsalted butter	4 oz
90 g	brown sugar	3 oz
1	lemon, finely chopped rind only	1
30 g	clear honey	1 oz
2	egg whites, lightly beaten	2
125 g	plain flour	4 oz
1 tsp	baking powder	1 tsp
2 tbsp	thickened loganberry purée (page 15)	2 tbsp
30 g	desiccated coconut	1 oz

Preheat the oven to 190°C (375°F or Mark 5). Butter 15 small, oval, fluted tartlet tins or deep round bun tins. Dust them lightly with flour.

Using a wooden spoon, beat the butter with the sugar, lemon rind and honey until soft and creamy. Beat in 1 tablespoon of warm water and continue beating until the mixture is very light and fluffy. Gradually beat in the egg whites. Sift the flour and baking powder into the creamed mixture, then fold in carefully with a metal spoon or rubber spatula.

Spoon half the mixture into the prepared tins and spread it evenly, then put a little of the loganberry purée in the centre of each bun. Divide the remaining creamed mixture among the tins and carefully spread it out to cover the loganberry purée. Put the tins on a baking sheet. Sprinkle the desiccated coconut evenly on top of the filled tins.

Bake the buns for 15 to 20 minutes, until they are well risen and springy to the touch. Allow them to cool in the tins for 2 to 3 minutes, then transfer them to wire racks to cool completely.

EDITOR'S NOTE: *The loganberry purée can be replaced with any other fruit purée or jam without added sugar.*

Spiced Teacakes

Makes 12 teacakes
Working time: about 50 minutes
Total time: about 2 hours and 40 minutes

Per teacake:
Calories **235**
Protein **6g**
Cholesterol **30mg**
Total fat **5g**
Saturated fat **3g**
Sodium **30mg**

250 g	plain flour	8 oz
½ tsp	salt	½ tsp
½ tsp	grated nutmeg	½ tsp
¼ tsp	ground cloves	¼ tsp
½ tsp	ground cinnamon	½ tsp
½ tsp	ground allspice	½ tsp
¼ tsp	ground mace	¼ tsp
250 g	wholemeal flour	8 oz
60 g	light brown sugar	2 oz
30 g	unsalted butter	1 oz
30 g	fresh yeast, or 15 g (½ oz) dried yeast	1 oz
1	egg, beaten	1
6 tbsp	soured cream	6 tbsp
60 g	currants	2 oz
60 g	sultanas	2 oz
2 tbsp	clear honey	2 tbsp

Sift the plain flour, salt and spices into a large bowl. Mix in the wholemeal flour and sugar. Rub the butter into the flours and make a well in the centre of the mixture. Dissolve the yeast in 15 cl (¼ pint) of tepid water; if using dried yeast, leave it to stand, following the manufacturer's instructions. Pour the yeast liquid into the centre of the flour and add the egg and soured cream. Mix to form a soft dough.

Knead the dough on a lightly floured surface for about 10 minutes, until it is smooth and elastic. Put the dough in a clean bowl. Cover the bowl with plastic film and leave it in a warm place for about 1 hour, until the dough has doubled in size. Meanwhile, butter and lightly flour three baking sheets.

Knock back the risen dough, then knead in the currants and sultanas. Divide the dough into 12 equal pieces. Knead and shape each piece into a smooth ball. Roll them with a rolling pin into flat rounds about 10 cm (4 inches) in diameter and place four on each baking sheet. Prick the rounds well with a fork.

Loosely cover the teacakes with plastic film and leave them in a warm place for about 30 minutes, until doubled in size. Meanwhile, preheat the oven to 220°C (425°F or Mark 7).

Bake the risen teacakes for 15 to 20 minutes, until they are golden-brown and sound hollow when lightly tapped on the base. Remove the teacakes from the oven and immediately brush them with honey. Leave them on wire racks to cool.

SUGGESTED ACCOMPANIMENT: *thickened fruit purée (page 15) or jam without added sugar.*

Rum Babas

THE BUTTERY YEAST CAKES KNOWN AS BABAS ARE TRADITIONALLY
SOAKED IN A VERY SWEET SYRUP AND ADORNED WITH CREAM. THIS
RECIPE SUBSTITUTES GREEK YOGURT FOR CREAM AND CUTS DOWN
ON BOTH THE BUTTER IN THE DOUGH AND THE SUGAR IN THE SYRUP.

Makes 12 babas
Working time: about 50 minutes
Total time: about 4 hours

Per baba:
Calories **175**
Protein **4g**
Cholesterol **30mg**
Total fat **4g**
Saturated fat **2g**
Sodium **90mg**

175 g	plain flour	6 oz
¼ tsp	salt	¼ tsp
15 g	caster sugar	½ oz
15 g	fresh yeast, or 7 g (¼ oz) dried yeast	½ oz
5 tbsp	skimmed milk, tepid	5 tbsp
1	egg	1
2	egg whites	2
1	orange, finely grated rind only	1
45 g	unsalted butter, softened	1½ oz
4 tbsp	thick Greek yogurt, well chilled	4 tbsp
3	oranges, rind and pith removed, flesh cut into segments (page 14)	3

Syrup

1	orange, strained juice only	1
90 g	light brown sugar	3 oz
125 g	clear honey	4 oz
4 tbsp	rum	4 tbsp

To make the dough, sift the flour, salt and caster sugar
into a bowl and make a well in the centre. Dissolve the
yeast in the milk; if using dried yeast, leave it to stand,
following the manufacturer's instructions. Beat the egg
and egg whites together. Pour the
yeast liquid and eggs into the
centre of the flour. Cover

the bowl with plastic film and leave it in a warm place
until the yeast begins to bubble — about 30 minutes.

Add the orange rind to the mixture and beat it well
for about 5 minutes, until it forms a smooth and elastic
dough. Cover the bowl again and leave the dough in a
warm place to rise until doubled in size — about 1
hour. Meanwhile, butter and lightly flour twelve 7.5 by
3 cm (3 by 1¼ inch) fluted moulds.

When the dough has reached the right volume,
gradually beat the softened butter into it. Divide the
mixture evenly among the prepared moulds. Place the
moulds on a baking sheet and leave them in a warm
place for 30 to 40 minutes, until the dough reaches the
top of the moulds. Meanwhile, preheat the oven to
200°C (400°F or Mark 6).

Bake the babas for 15 to 20 minutes, until golden-
brown, firm to the touch and slightly shrunk from the
sides of the moulds. Cool the babas in the moulds for
5 minutes, then transfer them to a wire rack and leave
them to reach room temperature.

While the babas are cooking, make the syrup. Put
the orange juice, brown sugar and honey into a
saucepan with 45 cl (¾ pint) of water. Heat gently
until the sugar is completely dissolved, stirring occasionally. Bring the syrup to the boil and boil it for 5
minutes until it becomes heavy. Stir in the rum.

Using a small, sharp, pointed knife, carefully cut a
cone from the centre of each baba. Place the cones
upside down on the rack next to the babas. Stand the
rack on a large tray. Spoon the warm syrup over the
babas and their centres, to drench them thoroughly.
Collect the syrup from the tray below and spoon it over
the babas repeatedly until it is all absorbed.

Spoon the chilled yogurt into the centre of each
baba, decorate each cake with the orange segments
and replace the centres.

EDITOR'S NOTE: *Whisky may be substituted for the rum.*

Carrot and Raisin Buns

Makes 18 buns
Working time: about 15 minutes
Total time: about 1 hour

Per bun:			
Calories **135**	250 g	carrots, peeled and grated	8 oz
Protein **2g**	2	eggs	2
Cholesterol **25mg**	12.5 cl	clear honey	4 fl oz
Total fat **8g**	12.5 cl	safflower oil	4 fl oz
Saturated fat **2g**	175 g	wholemeal flour	6 oz
Sodium **25mg**	2 tsp	baking powder	2 tsp
	1 tsp	ground cinnamon	1 tsp
	60 g	raisins	2 oz

Preheat the oven to 180°C (350°F or Mark 4). Grease and then lightly flour 18 bun tins.

Put the carrots in a bowl. Add the eggs, honey and safflower oil and mix them together with a fork. Sift the flour, baking powder and cinnamon into the bowl, adding the bran left in the sieve. Add the raisins. Using a wooden spoon, beat the flour mixture and raisins into the other ingredients.

Fill the bun tins three-quarters full with the carrot and raisin mixture and bake the buns for 20 minutes, until the centres spring back when pressed. Loosen the buns gently from the tins with a knife and transfer them to a wire rack to cool.

Fig Rings and Date Crescents

Makes 24 rings and 16 crescents
Working time: about 50 minutes
Total time: about 4 hours

Per ring:			
Calories **85**	500 g	plain flour	1 lb
Protein **2g**	½ tsp	salt	½ tsp
Cholesterol **5mg**	60 g	caster sugar	2 oz
Total fat **2g**	1	lemon, finely grated rind only	1
Saturated fat **1g**	125 g	unsalted butter	4 oz
Sodium **25mg**	30 g	fresh yeast, or 15g (½ oz) dried yeast	1 oz
	17.5 cl	skimmed milk, tepid	6 fl oz
	1	egg, beaten	1
	1	egg white	1
	2 tsp	icing sugar	2 tsp

	Fig filling		
175 g	dried figs	6 oz
1	lemon, finely grated rind only	1
1½ tbsp	fresh lemon juice	1½ tbsp
1 tbsp	clear honey	1 tbsp
	Date filling		
125 g	dried stoned dates	4 oz
1	orange, rind finely grated, juice strained	1
60 g	shelled walnuts, chopped	2 oz

Per crescent:
Calories **125**
Protein **3g**
Cholesterol **10mg**
Total fat **5g**
Saturated fat **2g**
Sodium **25mg**

Sift the flour and salt into a large bowl and add all but 1 teaspoon of the caster sugar. Mix in the lemon rind, then rub in the butter until the mixture resembles fine breadcrumbs. Dissolve the yeast in the tepid milk; if using dried yeast, leave it to stand, following the manufacturer's instructions. Pour the yeast liquid and the beaten egg into the flour and butter mixture and mix together to form a firm dough. Knead very lightly, on a floured surface, to smooth the dough. Put it in a clean bowl, cover the bowl with plastic film and refrigerate for 2 to 3 hours. (The period in the refrigerator makes the soft dough firm enough to handle and allows it to rise very slowly and gently.)

Meanwhile, prepare the fillings. To make the fig filling, put the dried figs, lemon rind, lemon juice and honey into a food processor and blend them to a smooth paste. Alternatively, very finely chop the figs, and mix them in a bowl with the remaining ingredients to make a paste. Cover the paste and set it aside.

To make the date filling, chop the dates and put them in a saucepan together with the orange rind and juice. Heat gently until the dates soften and absorb all of the orange juice. Remove the dates from the heat, mix in the chopped walnuts and allow the mixture to cool. Cover it and set it aside.

Preheat the oven to 200°C (400°F or Mark 6). Butter three baking sheets.

When the refrigeration time is up, remove half of the dough from the refrigerator to make the fig rings. Roll out the dough on a floured surface to a rectangle about 45 by 30 cm (18 by 12 inches). Trim the edges, then cut the rectangle lengthwise into three equal strips; cut each strip crosswise into eight equal pieces. Pipe the fig paste along one edge of each pastry dough piece, roll up the dough and form each roll into a ring, as demonstrated below, left. Place the rings on two of the baking sheets, with the lengthwise joins underneath. Leave the rings to stand in a warm place for about 15 minutes to rise a little.

Lightly mix the egg white with the reserved caster sugar. Brush half of the glaze evenly over the rings. Bake the rings for about 15 minutes until they are well risen and golden-brown.

To make the crescents, remove the remaining dough from the refrigerator and roll it out to about 5 mm (1/4 inch) thick. Cut out oval shapes from the dough and spread a heaped teaspoon of the date mixture down the middle of each oval *(below, right)*. Roll the ovals up to enclose the filling. Bend the dough into crescent shapes. Place them on the third baking sheet, with the joins underneath. Leave to stand in a warm place for about 15 minutes to rise a little. Then glaze and bake them in the same way as the rings.

Transfer the rings and crescents to wire racks to cool. Sift the icing sugar lightly over them. If possible, serve the rings and crescents just warm.

Shaping Rings and Crescents

1 *FILLING THE FIG RINGS. Using a piping bag fitted with a plain nozzle about 8 mm (3/8 inch) in diameter, pipe lines of fig paste along one long edge of each rectangle. Roll up the dough to enclose the paste, forming a cylinder with the join underneath. Bring the two ends round to meet each other, and pinch them together to create a circle.*

2 *ENCLOSING THE DATE STUFFING. Using a 10 cm (4 inch) oval cutter, cut ovals from the rolled dough. Place a heaped teaspoon of date mixture in the centre of each oval. Roll each oval lengthwise round its filling, keeping the ends pointed. Shape the dough into crescents and place them seam side down on the baking sheet.*

Fairy Cakes

Makes 12 cakes
Working time: about 30 minutes
Total time: 1 hour and 15 minutes

Per plain, cherry or sultana cake:			
	125 g	polyunsaturated margarine	4 oz
	60 g	caster sugar	2 oz
	60 g	clear honey	2 oz
	1 tsp	pure vanilla extract	1 tsp
	2	egg whites, lightly beaten	2
	175 g	plain flour	6 oz
	1½ tsp	baking powder	1½ tsp
	15 g	glacé cherries, chopped	½ oz
	15 g	desiccated coconut	½ oz
	30 g	sultanas	1 oz
	15 cl	pastry cream (page 16)	¼ pint
	1	hazelnut, thinly sliced	1
		chocolate curls for garnish (page 19)	

Per plain, cherry or
sultana cake:
Calories **195**
Protein **2g**
Cholesterol **25mg**
Total fat **8g**
Saturated fat **2g**
Sodium **160mg**

Per coconut cake:
Calories **205**
Protein **3g**
Cholesterol **25mg**
Total fat **12g**
Saturated fat **5g**
Sodium **155mg**

Preheat the oven to 190°C (375°F or Mark 5). Grease and lightly flour 12 deep, sloping-sided bun tins.

Put the margarine, sugar and honey in a bowl. With a wooden spoon, beat them until they are soft and creamy. Beat in the vanilla extract with 3 tablespoons of warm water; continue beating until the mixture be-

comes very light and fluffy. Gradually beat in the egg whites. Sift the flour and baking powder over the creamed mixture, then fold them in carefully with a metal spoon or rubber spatula.

Half fill three of the bun tins with the plain mixture. Divide the remaining mixture equally into three. To one third add the cherries, reserving three pieces; to another third add the coconut, reserving 2 teaspoons; to the remaining third, add the sultanas. Spoon the mixtures into the bun tins. Bake for 10 to 15 minutes until the fairy cakes are well risen, golden-brown and springy to the touch. Leave them in the tins for 2 to 3 minutes, then transfer them to wire racks.

When the cakes have cooled, put the pastry cream into a piping bag fitted with a medium-sized star nozzle. Pipe a shell shape on top of each cake. Decorate the plain cakes with the hazelnut slices, the cherry cakes with the reserved cherry pieces, the coconut cakes with the reserved coconut, and the sultana cakes with the chocolate curls.

Madeleines

THIS RECIPE FOR THE SHELL-SHAPED SPONGE CAKES KNOWN
AS MADELEINES USES LESS EGG YOLK AND BUTTER THAN MORE
TRADITIONAL MIXTURES.

Makes 20 madeleines
Working time: about 10 minutes
Total time: about 35 minutes

Per madeleine:
Calories **65**
Protein **1g**
Cholesterol **30mg**
Total fat **2 g**
Saturated fat **1g**
Sodium **10mg**

1	egg	1
1	egg white	1
90 g	caster sugar	3 oz
1 tbsp	amaretto liqueur	1 tbsp
90 g	plain flour	3 oz
45 g	unsalted butter, melted and cooled	1½ oz
1 tbsp	vanilla sugar	1 tbsp

Preheat the oven to 200°C (400°F or Mark 6). Butter twenty 7.5 cm (3 inch) madeleine moulds and dust them lightly with flour.

Put the egg and egg white into a bowl with the caster sugar and amaretto. Whisk the mixture until it thickens to the consistency of unwhipped double cream. Sift the flour lightly over the surface of the mixture, then fold it in very carefully with a metal spoon or rubber spatula. Gently fold in the melted butter.

Half fill each madeleine mould with mixture. Bake the madeleines for 15 to 20 minutes, until well risen, lightly browned and springy to the touch. Carefully turn them out of the moulds on to a wire rack and immediately sift the vanilla sugar over them. Serve the madeleines while still warm, or allow them to cool.

Raspberry-Filled Shells

Makes 18 shells
Working time: about 40 minutes
Total time: about 1 hour and 40 minutes

Per shell:		
Calories **107**	3	eggs	3
Protein **2g**	90 g	caster sugar	3 oz
Cholesterol **50mg**	90 g	plain flour	3 oz
Total fat **6g**	¼ litre	whipping cream, whipped	8 fl oz
Saturated fat **3g**	350 g	fresh raspberries, or	12 oz
Sodium **20mg**		frozen raspberries, thawed	
	1 tbsp	icing sugar	1 tbsp

Preheat the oven to 180°C (350°F or Mark 4). Grease 18 rounded, shell-patterned bun moulds and dust the moulds lightly with flour.

To make the sponge, put the eggs and caster sugar in a large bowl. Place the bowl over a saucepan of hot, but not boiling, water on a low heat. Whisk until the mixture becomes thick and very pale in colour *(page 12)*. Remove the bowl from the heat and continue whisking until the mixture is cool and will hold a ribbon trail almost indefinitely. Sift the flour very lightly over the top of the whisked mixture and fold it in carefully with a large metal spoon or a rubber spatula.

Divide the sponge batter equally among the 18 bun moulds and spread it evenly. Bake the sponges for 25 to 30 minutes until very well risen, lightly browned and springy to the touch. Turn the sponges out of the moulds on to a wire rack to cool, rounded sides up.

Cut each sponge in half, at a slight angle to the horizontal. Cover the bottom halves with cream and raspberries and set the top halves on the filling at an angle, so that the cakes resemble half-open clams. Sift the icing sugar over the cakes.

Pistachio, Coconut and Walnut Shapes

Makes 12 shapes
Working time: about 1 hour
Total time: about 2 hours

Per shape:		
Calories **130**	2	eggs	2
Protein **4g**	1	egg white	1
Cholesterol **45mg**	90 g	caster sugar	3 oz
Total fat **9g**	90 g	plain flour	3 oz
Saturated fat **3g**	30 g	unsalted butter, melted	1 oz
Sodium **20mg**		and cooled	
	350 g	apricot jam without added	12 oz
		sugar	
	45 g	shelled pistachio nuts, skinned	1½ oz
		and finely chopped	
	20 g	desiccated coconut	¾ oz
	45 g	shelled walnuts, finely	1½ oz
		chopped	
	2 tsp	icing sugar	2 tsp

Preheat the oven to 180°C (350°F or Mark 4). Butter a 28 by 18 by 3 cm (11 by 7 by 1¼ inches) oblong tin and line the base with non-stick parchment paper.

Put the eggs, egg white and caster sugar in a mixing bowl. Place the bowl over a saucepan of hot, but not boiling, water on a low heat. Whisk the eggs and sugar together by hand or with an electric mixer until thick and very pale *(page 12)*. Remove the bowl from the saucepan and continue whisking until the mixture is cool and will hold a ribbon trail almost indefinitely. Sift the flour very lightly over the surface of the whisked mixture, then fold it in gently using a large metal spoon or rubber spatula. Gradually fold in the melted butter.

Pour the sponge mixture into the prepared tin and spread it evenly. Bake the sponge for 20 to 25 minutes, until well risen, springy to the touch and very slightly shrunk from the sides of the tin. Carefully turn the sponge on to a wire rack. Loosen the baking paper but do not remove it. Place another rack on top of the paper, then invert both racks together so that the paper is underneath. Remove the top rack and leave the sponge to cool.

Transfer the sponge to a flat surface. Cut it in half horizontally. Spread the bottom layer with 2 table-spoons of the apricot jam. Place the second layer on top of the first and press the two layers firmly together. Trim the crisp edges from the sponge.

Cut a 4.5 cm (1 ¾ inch) wide strip from one of the long sides of the sponge; cut four squares from the strip. Using a 6 cm (2½ inch) plain round cutter and a 7 cm (2 ¾ inch) star cutter, cut out four rounds and four stars from the remaining sponge.

Warm the remaining apricot jam in a small sauce-pan. Sieve it, then return it to the pan and bring it to the boil. Taking one piece of sponge at a time, spear the shapes on a fork and brush them evenly with the hot jam. Paint on only a thin layer of jam: too much would make the sponge soggy. Taking each shape in

turn in one hand, sprinkle and press nuts evenly over its surface with the other hand. Coat the rounds with the pistachio nuts, the stars with the desiccated coconut, and the squares with the walnuts.

Rest a sheet of paper diagonally across each walnut square in turn, so as to cover half of the square. Sift icing sugar over the exposed halves of the walnut squares and over the pistachio rounds.

EDITOR'S NOTE: *To skin pistachio nuts, parboil them for 1 minute, drain them, then enfold them in a towel and rub briskly to loosen the skins.*

Pineapple Rondels

Makes 12 rondels
Working time: about 1 hour and 30 minutes
Total time: about 2 hours

Per rondel:			
Calories **250**	3	eggs	3
Protein **5g**	1	egg white	1
Cholesterol **70mg**	125 g	vanilla-flavoured caster sugar	4 oz
Total fat **6g**	125 g	plain flour	4 oz
Saturated fat **1g**	1	medium pineapple, skin and eyes removed	1
Sodium **35mg**	3	large oranges, skin and pith sliced off (page 14)	3
	125 g	granulated sugar	4 oz
	30 cl	orange-flavoured pastry cream (page 16)	½ pint
	90 g	shelled walnuts, finely chopped	3 oz

Preheat the oven to 180°C (350°F or Mark 4). Grease a 38 by 28 by 2 cm (15 by 11 by ¾ inch) baking tin and line it with non-stick parchment paper.

To make the sponge bases for the rondels, put the eggs and egg white in a large bowl with the caster sugar. By hand or using an electric mixer, whisk the eggs and sugar for 5 to 6 minutes over a pan of hot,

but not boiling, water on a low heat, until it becomes thick and very pale *(page 12)*. Remove the bowl from the saucepan and continue whisking until the mixture is cool and will hold a ribbon trail. Sift the flour very lightly over the top of the mixture and carefully fold it in with a metal spoon or a rubber spatula. Pour the batter into the prepared tin and spread it evenly. Bake for 25 to 30 minutes, until the sponge is well risen, lightly browned and springy to the touch.

Turn the sponge on to a large wire rack and loosen the paper but do not remove it. Place another rack on top, then invert the racks together so the paper is underneath: if the sponge rested directly on the rack, it would stick to the metal. Allow the sponge to cool.

Meanwhile, cut the pineapple into 12 equal slices. Remove the hard centre core from each slice with a small plain cutter. Trim the slices into neat rings, using an 8 cm (3¼ inch) cutter as a guide.

Remove the two ends of each orange and slice the remainder crosswise to create four uniform slices. Heat 60 g (2 oz) of the granulated sugar with 15 cl (¼ pint) of water in a wide, shallow pan. When the sugar dissolves, bring the syrup to the boil and simmer for 3 minutes. Poach the pineapple and orange slices, in batches, in the sugar syrup for about 2 minutes — just long enough to soften them slightly. Lift the slices from the syrup with a slotted spoon and transfer them to a wire rack to drain. Boil the remaining syrup to reduce its volume by about half.

Transfer the cooled sponge and its paper to a board. Using an 8 cm (3¼ inch) plain round cutter, cut 12 rounds from the sponge cake. Brush each round with the reduced syrup.

Spread each round of sponge with the orange-flavoured pastry cream, coating the top and sides evenly. Cover the sides only with the chopped walnuts. Lift the rounds off the paper on to a large foil-lined baking sheet. Place a slice of pineapple and a slice of orange on each coated sponge round.

To make caramel for a garnish, gently heat the remaining granulated sugar in a small pan with 3 tablespoons of cold water. Stir the syrup and brush the sides of the pan with hot water from time to time. When every granule of sugar has dissolved, bring the syrup to the boil and cook until it turns golden-brown.

Very lightly oil two baking sheets. Allow the caramel to cool slightly, then trickle it in fine lines from a small spoon across the baking sheets. The caramel will set within seconds. Break it in pieces and pile the fragments on top of each cake.

Strawberry Galettes

Makes 12 galettes
Working time: about 1 hour
Total time: about 2 hours and 10 minutes

Per galette:
Calories **185**
Protein **6g**
Cholesterol **95mg**
Total fat **7g**
Saturated fat **3g**
Sodium **80mg**

4	eggs	4
1	egg white	1
150 g	caster sugar	5 oz
150 g	plain flour	5 oz
60 g	unsalted butter, melted and cooled	2 oz
15 cl	double cream	¼ pint
1 tsp	pure vanilla extract	1 tsp
2 tbsp	icing sugar	2 tbsp
200 g	fromage frais	7 oz
500 g	strawberries, hulled, all but six sliced	1 lb

Preheat the oven to 180°C (350°F or Mark 4). Butter a 38 by 28 by 2 cm (15 by 11 by ¾ inch) oblong baking tin. Line the base with non-stick parchment paper.

Put the eggs and egg white into a large mixing bowl with the sugar. Place the bowl over a saucepan of hot, but not boiling, water on a low heat. Whisk the eggs and sugar by hand or with an electric mixer until they become thick and very pale *(page 12)*. Remove the bowl from the heat and continue whisking until the mixture is cool and will hold a ribbon trail almost indefinitely. Very lightly sift the flour over the surface of the egg mixture, then fold it in carefully with a large metal spoon or a rubber spatula. Gradually fold the melted butter into the mixture.

Pour the sponge mixture into the prepared baking tin and spread it evenly. Bake the sponge for 30 to 35 minutes until risen, lightly browned and springy to the touch. Turn it out of the tin on to a cooling rack and loosen but do not remove the paper. Place another cooling rack on top of the paper and invert both racks together so that the paper is underneath. Remove the top rack and allow the sponge to cool.

To make the filling, put the double cream, vanilla extract and 1 tablespoon of the icing sugar into a bowl and whisk them until the cream is thick but not buttery. Gently mix in the *fromage frais*. Keep the cream filling refrigerated until you use it.

Transfer the cooled sponge to a flat surface. Using an 8 cm (3¼ inch) plain round cutter, cut out 12 rounds from the sponge. Slice each round in half horizontally; then cut each top round into six equal triangles.

Spoon the cream filling into a piping bag fitted with a small star nozzle. Pipe three quarters of the cream filling on to the bottom rounds and cover it with the sliced strawberries. Pipe six evenly spaced rosettes of cream on top of each strawberry-covered round. Halve the reserved strawberries and slice each half into six slices. Support a triangle of sponge at an angle against each rosette of cream and slip the reserved strawberry slices between the sponge triangles. Sift the remaining icing sugar lightly over the galettes.

Lemon Marzipan Discs

Makes 12 discs
Working time: about 1 hour and 15 minutes
Total time: about 2 hours and 15 minutes

Per disc:
Calories **300**
Protein **6g**
Cholesterol **60mg**
Total fat **15g**
Saturated fat **3g**
Sodium **90mg**

3	eggs	3
1	egg white	1
125 g	caster sugar	4 oz
1	lemon, finely grated rind only	1
125 g	plain flour	4 oz
30 g	unsalted butter, melted and cooled	1 oz
2 tbsp	apricot jam without added sugar, heated and sieved	2 tbsp
12	pairs of grapes, sugared (page 18)	12
Marzipan		
90 g	ground almonds	3 oz
90 g	icing sugar, sifted	3 oz
1	lemon, finely grated rind only	1
2 tsp	fresh lemon juice	2 tsp
1	small egg white, lightly whisked	1
1 tsp	caster sugar	1 tsp
Lemon cream		
60 g	polyunsaturated margarine	2 oz
2 tsp	fresh lemon juice	2 tsp
1	egg white	1
60 g	caster sugar	2 oz

Preheat the oven to 180°C (350°F or Mark 4). Butter an oblong tin about 30 by 20 by 4 cm (12 by 8 by 1½ inches). Line the base with non-stick parchment paper.

Put the eggs, egg white, caster sugar and lemon rind into a mixing bowl. Place the bowl over a saucepan of hot, but not boiling, water on a low heat. Whisk the eggs and sugar together by hand or with an electric mixer until thick and very pale *(page 12)*. Remove the bowl from the saucepan and continue whisking until the mixture is cool and will hold a ribbon trail almost indefinitely. Sift the flour very lightly over the surface of the whisked mixture, then fold it in gently using a large metal spoon or a rubber spatula. Gradually fold in the melted butter.

Pour the sponge mixture into the prepared tin and spread it evenly. Bake it for 25 to 30 minutes, until well risen, springy to the touch and very lightly shrunk from the sides of the tin. Carefully turn the sponge cake on to a cooling rack. Loosen the baking paper but do not remove it. Place another cooling rack on top of the paper, then invert both racks together so that the paper is underneath. Remove the top rack and allow the sponge to cool.

To make the marzipan, mix the ground almonds with the sifted icing sugar and grated lemon rind in a bowl. Add the lemon juice and about one third of the whisked egg white — enough to make a stiff paste; reserve the remaining egg white for another use. Very lightly knead the marzipan until it is smooth. Wrap the marzipan in plastic film and refrigerate it while making the lemon cream.

To prepare the lemon cream, beat the margarine and lemon juice together in a bowl. Put the egg white and caster sugar into another bowl and place the bowl over a saucepan of hot, but not boiling, water on a low heat. Whisk the egg white and sugar together until they form a stiff, shiny meringue. Then, very gradually, beat the meringue into the margarine and lemon juice to make a fluffy cream.

On a surface very lightly sifted with icing sugar, roll out the marzipan to a rectangle a little larger than 30 by 18 cm (12 by 7 inches). Mark the marzipan with a ridged rolling pin, rolling from one short end. Trim the edges, then sprinkle the marzipan evenly with the teaspoon of caster sugar. Cut across the rectangle to make twelve 2.5 cm (1 inch) wide strips.

Transfer the cooled sponge to a flat surface. Using a 6 cm (2½ inch) plain round cutter, cut out 12 sponge discs. Spread the top of each sponge generously with lemon cream. Turn each of the marzipan strips over and lightly brush the smooth side with the apricot jam. Wrap each marzipan strip round a sponge disc with the jam side to the sponge. Press the marzipan gently into position and trim it to fit exactly. Decorate the lemon marzipan discs with the sugared grapes.

Lemon Curd Cakes

Serves 12
Working time: about 45 minutes
Total time: about 1 hour and 45 minutes

Calories **170**			
Protein **2g**	3	eggs	3
Cholesterol **60mg**	1	egg white	1
Total fat **4g**	125 g	caster sugar	4 oz
Saturated fat **2g**	125 g	plain flour	4 oz
Sodium **25mg**	30 g	unsalted butter, melted and cooled	1 oz
	3 tbsp	lemon curd (page 15)	3 tbsp
	Piped frosting		
	250 g	caster sugar	8 oz
	1	egg white	1

Preheat the oven to 180°C (350°F or Mark 4). Grease an oblong tin about 28 by 18 by 4 cm (11 by 7 by 1½ inches). Line the base with non-stick parchment paper.

Put the eggs, egg white and caster sugar in a large bowl. Place the bowl over a saucepan of hot, but not boiling, water on a low heat. Whisk the eggs and sugar by hand or with an electric mixer until thick and very pale *(page 12)*. Remove the bowl from the heat and continue whisking until the mixture is cool and will hold a ribbon trail almost indefinitely. Sift the flour very lightly over the top of the whisked mixture and fold it in carefully with a large metal spoon or rubber spatula. Gradually fold in the melted butter.

Pour the sponge mixture into the prepared tin and spread it evenly. Bake the sponge for 25 to 30 minutes, until well risen, firm to the touch and very slightly shrunk away from the sides of the tin. Turn the sponge out on to a wire rack. Loosen but do not remove the parchment paper. Place another rack on top of the paper, then invert both the racks together so that the paper is underneath. Remove the top rack and leave the sponge to cool. Transfer the sponge on to a flat surface. Slice it in half horizontally and sandwich the two layers together with lemon curd.

To make the frosting, put the sugar in a saucepan with 7.5 cl (2½ fl oz) of cold water. Heat very gently until every granule of sugar has dissolved, brushing the sides of the pan down with hot water from time to time. Bring the syrup to the boil and cook it until its temperature reads 116°C (240°F) on a sugar thermometer. Meanwhile, whisk the egg white until it is very stiff but not dry. Immediately the sugar syrup reaches the required temperature, whisk the syrup into the egg white, pouring it in a steady stream from a height. Continue whisking until the frosting just loses its shine and becomes stiff enough to hold a peak.

Without delay, since the frosting begins to harden within a few minutes, spoon the frosting into a piping bag fitted with a seven-point 8 mm (5⁄16 inch) star nozzle. Pipe the frosting in diagonal lines across the cake. Pipe rows of stars between the lines. Slice the sponge into 12 when the frosting has set.

Chestnut and Chocolate Baskets

Makes 12 cakes
Working time: about 1 hour and 10 minutes
Total time: about 3 hours

Per cake:
Calories **230**
Protein **4g**
Cholesterol **60mg**
Total fat **8g**
Saturated fat **4g**
Sodium **30mg**

325 g	chestnut purée	11 oz
3	eggs, separated	3
175 g	caster sugar	6 oz
250 g	plain chocolate	8 oz
1	egg white	1
2 tbsp	rum	2 tbsp
180 g	thick Greek yogurt	6 oz
1 tsp	icing sugar	1 tsp

Preheat the oven to 180°C (350°F or Mark 4). Grease twelve 10 cm (4 inch) tartlet tins and line the base of each with a round of non-stick parchment paper.

Whisk the chestnut purée, egg yolks and 125 g (4 oz) of the caster sugar in a large bowl until the mixture becomes very pale and thick. Melt 90 g (3 oz) of the chocolate in a bowl over a pan of hot water. Let it cool but not set, then whisk it into the chestnut mixture.

In another bowl, whisk the whites until stiff but not dry. Whisk in the remaining sugar to make meringue, and gradually fold this into the chestnut mixture.

Divide the chestnut mixture equally among the prepared tins and spread it evenly. Place the tins on baking trays. Bake the chestnut sponges for 15 to 20 minutes, until they are well risen and firm to the touch; a wooden cocktail stick should come out clean when inserted in the centre. Allow them to cool in the tins.

Chop 90 g (3 oz) of the remaining chocolate. Put it in a small bowl with the rum. Place the bowl over a saucepan of hot, but not boiling, water and stir until the chocolate melts and is smoothly blended with the rum. Remove the mixture from the heat. When it has cooled but not set, fold in the yogurt.

Carefully remove the chestnut sponges from their tins and peel off the parchment paper. (If you used fluted tartlet tins, straighten the sides by trimming the sponges with a plain round cutter.) Place the sponge rounds, well spaced, on foil-lined baking sheets. Spread the chocolate cream over the tops of the chestnut bases. Refrigerate the cakes until firm.

To make a paper-thin chocolate wall for each cake, cut out 12 strips of non-stick parchment paper, 2.5 cm (1 inch) wide and long enough to fit round the chocolate bases with an overlap of about 1 cm (½ inch). Melt the remaining chocolate and use a small palette knife to spread the chocolate thinly over one strip of paper at a time, leaving 1 cm (½ inch) clear at one end for handling. Carefully wrap the paper strip, chocolate side to cake, round each of the bases.

Thinly spread any remaining chocolate on a marble slab or smooth work surface. When the chocolate is no longer sticky to the touch, scrape it off the slab with a knife, held at an angle, to form shavings. Sprinkle the shavings over the top of the chocolate cream. Refrigerate the cakes until the chocolate is firmly set — about 1 hour — then carefully peel away the paper. Sift the icing sugar lightly over the surfaces. Chill the cakes until they are served.

EDITOR'S NOTE: *To make 325 g (11 oz) of purée from fresh chestnuts, slit 650 g (22 oz) of nuts down one side, parboil them for 1 to 2 minutes, shell and peel them. Simmer them for about 20 minutes until tender, then drain and sieve them.*

Chocolate Sponges Coated in Coffee Cream

Makes 10 sponges
Working time: about 1 hour and 15 minutes
Total time: about 2 hours and 15 minutes

Per sponge:
Calories **210**
Protein **4g**
Cholesterol **80mg**
Total fat **10g**
Saturated fat **5g**
Sodium **40mg**

3	eggs	3
1	egg white	1
125 g	caster sugar	4 oz
100 g	plain flour	3½ oz
15 g	cocoa powder	½ oz
90 g	plain chocolate, coarsely grated	3 oz
20	chocolate rose leaves (page 19)	20
Coffee cream		
60 g	unsalted butter	2 oz
1	egg white	1
90 g	caster sugar	3 oz
1 tbsp	strong black coffee, cooled	1 tbsp

Preheat the oven to 180°C (350°F or Mark 4). Butter a 30 by 20 by 4 cm (12 by 8 by 1½ inch) oblong tin. Line the base with non-stick parchment paper.

Put the eggs, egg white and caster sugar in a mixing bowl. Place the bowl over a saucepan of hot, but not boiling, water on a low heat. Whisk the eggs and sugar by hand or with an electric mixer until thick and very pale *(page 12)*. Remove the bowl from the saucepan and continue whisking until the mixture is cool and will hold a ribbon trail almost indefinitely. Sift the flour and

cocoa very lightly over the surface of the whisked mixture and fold them in gently, using a large metal spoon or a rubber spatula.

Pour the sponge mixture into the prepared tin and spread it evenly. Bake the sponge for 25 to 30 minutes, until well risen, springy to the touch and very slightly shrunk from the sides of the tin. Carefully turn the sponge cake on to a wire rack. Loosen the baking paper but do not remove it. Place another rack on top of the paper, then invert both racks together so that the paper is underneath. Remove the top rack and leave the sponge cake to cool.

To make the coffee cream, put the butter into a mixing bowl and beat well until it is light and fluffy. Put the egg white and caster sugar in another mixing bowl and place the bowl over a saucepan of hot, but not boiling, water. Using a hand whisk or an electric beater, whisk the egg white and sugar together until they form a stiff, shiny meringue. Gradually whisk the meringue into the butter to make a soft, fluffy cream, then gradually beat in the coffee.

Transfer the cooled sponge to a flat surface. Using an 8 cm (3¼ inch) plain oval cutter, cut out 10 ovals from the sponge. Take one oval at a time and spread the top with coffee cream. Mark a ridged pattern in the cream with a small palette knife or a fork. Spread the sides of each oval with a thin layer of coffee cream, then press the grated chocolate against the sides. Decorate the sponges with the chocolate rose leaves, each secured with a dab of coffee cream.

Mango Slices

Serves 16
Working time: about 1 hour and 15 minutes
Total time: about 5 hours

Calories **107**
Protein **3g**
Cholesterol **45mg**
Total fat **3g**
Saturated fat **1g**
Sodium **50mg**

3	eggs	3
1	egg white	1
90 g	caster sugar	3 oz
125 g	plain flour	4 oz
30 g	unsalted butter, melted and cooled	1 oz
1 tsp	powdered gelatine	1 tsp
¼ litre	thickened raspberry purée (page 15)	8 fl oz
2 tbsp	icing sugar	2 tbsp
Mango custard filling		
2	large ripe mangoes	2
4 tsp	powdered gelatine	4 tsp
30 g	cornflour	1 oz
30 cl	skimmed milk	½ pint
30 g	caster sugar	1 oz
1 tsp	pure vanilla extract	1 tsp
1	egg white	1

Preheat the oven to 180°C (350°F or Mark 4). Butter an oblong tin about 30 by 20 by 4 cm (12 by 8 by 1½ inches). Line the base with non-stick parchment paper.

To make the sponge, put the eggs, egg white and caster sugar in a mixing bowl. Place the bowl over a saucepan of hot, but not boiling, water on a low heat. Whisk the eggs and sugar together by hand or with an electric mixer until thick and very pale (page 12). Remove the bowl from the saucepan and continue whisking until the mixture is cool and will hold a ribbon trail almost indefinitely. Sift the flour very lightly over the surface of the whisked mixture, then fold it in gently, using a large metal spoon or a rubber spatula. Gradually fold in the melted butter.

Pour the sponge mixture into the prepared tin and spread it evenly. Bake for 20 to 25 minutes, until the sponge is well risen, springy to the touch and very slightly shrunk from the sides of the tin. Carefully turn the cake on to a wire rack. Loosen the baking paper but do not remove it. Place another rack on top of the paper, then invert both racks together so that the paper is underneath. Remove the top rack and leave the sponge cake to cool completely.

Line the base and short sides of an oblong baking tin, about 28 by 18 by 3 cm (11 by 7 by 1¼ inches),

with a double-thickness strip of aluminium foil, allowing it to overlap at the ends.

Put 2 teaspoons of cold water in a cup and sprinkle the gelatine evenly over the surface; leave the cup for a few minutes until the gelatine swells, absorbing all the water. Warm the raspberry purée in a pan, add the gelatine and stir until it has completely dissolved. Allow the purée to cool a little.

Transfer the sponge to a flat surface. Cut it in half horizontally. Place the bottom layer in the tin, trimming it to fit exactly. Set the top layer aside. Spread the raspberry purée evenly over the sponge in the tin, then refrigerate it while making the mango filling.

To make the mango filling, remove the peel from the mangoes, then cut the flesh away from the stones. Purée the flesh in a food processor or blender; you should have about ½ litre (16 fl oz). Put 3 tablespoons of cold water into a small bowl, then sprinkle the gelatine evenly over the surface. Leave the gelatine while making the custard.

In a bowl, blend the cornflour with a little of the milk. Pour the remaining milk into a saucepan and bring it to the boil. Stir the boiling milk into the cornflour, then pour it back into the saucepan. Bring the custard back to the boil, stirring continuously. Reduce the heat and cook gently, still stirring, until every trace of raw cornflour has gone. Stir in the sugar, vanilla extract and gelatine, and continue stirring until the gelatine has dissolved completely. Stir in the mango purée.

Whisk the egg white until it forms soft peaks, and fold it into the mango mixture. Pour the mango custard on top of the raspberry purée and spread it evenly. Place the remaining layer of sponge on top of the mango filling, trimming it to fit exactly. Refrigerate the cake for about 3 hours, until the filling is firmly set.

Loosen the mango custard from the sides of the tin with a small knife. With the aid of the overlapping foil strip, carefully lift the cake from the tin on to a board. If necessary, trim the sides to neaten them.

Leave two or three long skewers over a gas flame or on an electric ring for 5 minutes to become red hot. Meanwhile, cut the sponge slice in half lengthwise, then equally into eight crosswise to make 16 slices. Sift the icing sugar evenly over the slices. Before separating the slices, caramelize the icing sugar in a lattice pattern with the hot skewers (page 18).

4 *An Austrian kugelhopf (recipe, opposite) has cooked to a uniform texture thanks to its traditional ring shape, which allows microwaves to penetrate evenly.*

Cakes from the Microwave

The microwave oven not only bakes cakes quickly but also speeds up many steps in the preparation of their ingredients, from precooking fruit to melting fat. The recipes in this chapter, ranging from moist gingerbread squares to airy coconut sponges, demonstrate the versatility of the microwave oven for cake-making.

The results are not quite like those achieved in a conventional oven, since the surface of a microwaved cake never browns and crisps; a cake made with light-coloured ingredients remains pale. Although the dark ingredients — molasses, dates, wholemeal flour — in many recipes disguise the absence of surface colour, the cakes still lack the crusty top and sides of their conventionally baked equivalents. Microwave dishes are never floured as a preliminary to cooking; this step helps the browning process in a conventional oven but would leave a damp, grey coating on a microwaved cake. In place of flour, biscuit crumbs are used to line dishes in several of these recipes.

For making roulades, the absence of brittle edges is a real boon; the hard edges of conventionally baked sponges have to be trimmed before they can be rolled, lest they buckle. The chocolate and apricot roulade on page 138 and the raspberry and hazelnut roulade on page 139 demonstrate the professional results that a microwave oven gives.

One drawback of cakes without a crisp, dry surface is that their appearance can deceive. Because the top of a microwaved cake still looks wet at the end of the cooking time, the unwary may be inclined to return it to the oven to overcook. Resist the temptation: the cake will dry out in seconds.

The recipes have been tested in 650-watt and 700-watt ovens. Though power settings may vary among different ovens, the recipes use "high" to indicate 100 per cent power, "medium" for 50 per cent power and "defrost" for 30 per cent power. All recipes give instructions for turning the cakes so that they rise evenly; if your microwave oven has a revolving turntable, ignore these directions.

Sultana Kugelhopf

Serves 20
Working time: about 30 minutes
Total time: about 2 hours and 30 minutes

Calories **240**
Protein **6g**
Cholesterol **70mg**
Total fat **11g**
Saturated fat **4g**
Sodium **180mg**

60 g	digestive biscuits, crushed	2 oz
15	blanched almonds	15
30 cl	skimmed milk	½ pint
30 g	fresh yeast, or 15 g (½ oz) dried yeast	1 oz
30 g	caster sugar	1 oz
500 g	plain flour	1 lb
90 g	unsalted butter	3 oz
90 g	polyunsaturated margarine	3 oz
3	large eggs, beaten	3
½ tsp	salt	½ tsp
90 g	sultanas	3 oz
60 g	raisins	2 oz
30 g	currants	1 oz
1	lemon, grated rind only	1
	icing sugar	

Grease a 22 cm (9 inch) kugelhopf mould and sprinkle the mould evenly with the biscuit crumbs. Arrange the almonds on the base.

Pour the milk into a jug and microwave it on high for 1 minute or until tepid. Stir the fresh yeast into the milk; or reconstitute the dried yeast with the milk according to the manufacturer's instructions, adding 1 teaspoon of the caster sugar. Put 175 g (6 oz) of the flour in a bowl and gradually beat in the milk and yeast mixture. Cover the batter loosely with plastic film and microwave it at defrost for 1½ to 2 minutes. Leave to stand until well risen and frothy — 10 to 15 minutes.

Place the butter and margarine in a bowl and melt them by microwaving on high for 1 to 1½ minutes. Add the melted butter and margarine to the risen batter, together with the remaining sugar and flour, the eggs and salt. Beat the mixture well with a wooden spoon. Stir in the sultanas, raisins, currants and lemon rind and spoon the batter into the prepared mould.

Cover the batter loosely with plastic film and microwave it on defrost for 8 to 9 minutes, or until the batter has risen to the top of the mould. Leave the mixture to stand for 10 minutes, then microwave it, uncovered, on high for 6 minutes, giving the dish a quarter turn three times. Leave the kugelhopf to stand for 5 minutes before turning it out on a wire rack to cool. Before serving the kugelhopf, sprinkle it with icing sugar.

Coconut Sponges

Makes 12 sponges
Working time: about 30 minutes
Total time: about 50 minutes

Per sponge:
Calories **165**
Protein **3g**
Cholesterol **50mg**
Total fat **8g**
Saturated fat **5g**
Sodium **50mg**

60 g	unsalted butter	2 oz
125 g	caster sugar	4 oz
4 tbsp	skimmed milk	4 tbsp
2	eggs, beaten	2
125 g	plain flour	4 oz
1½ tsp	baking powder	1½ tsp
60 g	desiccated coconut	2 oz
4 tbsp	raspberry jam without added sugar	4 tbsp
2	glacé cherries, sliced	2
	angelica, cut into 12 small leaf shapes	

Grease the cups of a six-cup microwave muffin tray. In a mixing bowl, cream the butter with the caster sugar; beat in the skimmed milk and eggs. Sift the flour with the baking powder and fold them into the creamed mixture. Divide half of the mixture evenly between the cups and level the surfaces.

Microwave the cakes on high for 2 minutes, giving the tray a quarter turn three times. When cooked, the sponges will still be slightly moist on the surface. Leave them to stand for 5 minutes before turning them out on to a wire rack to cool. Microwave the other half of the sponge mixture in the same way.

Trim the bases of the cakes, if necessary, so that they stand steady. Spread the desiccated coconut in a shallow dish.

Put the jam in a bowl and microwave it on high for 30 seconds. Sieve the jam, then microwave it on high again for 15 seconds to warm it. Spear each sponge in turn on a fork, brush its top and sides with jam, then roll it in the coconut. Top each sponge with a slice of cherry and an angelica leaf.

Blackcurrant Muffins

Makes 18 muffins
Working time: about 30 minutes
Total time: about 50 minutes

Per muffin:
Calories **130**
Protein **2 g**
Cholesterol **20mg**
Total fat **5g**
Saturated fat **1g**
Sodium **80mg**

175 g	fresh blackcurrants, topped and tailed, or frozen blackcurrants, thawed	6 oz
1 tbsp	caster sugar	1 tbsp
175 g	malted wheat flour	6 oz
1½ tsp	baking powder	1½ tsp
6 tbsp	skimmed milk	6 tbsp
125 g	light brown sugar	4 oz
6 tbsp	safflower oil	6 tbsp
1	large egg, beaten	1
Golden topping		
4 tbsp	light brown sugar	4 tbsp
½ tsp	ground cinnamon	½ tsp

Put the blackcurrants and caster sugar in a bowl. Cover them loosely and microwave them on high for 1½ to 2 minutes until tender but still intact, stirring once. If microwaved for too long, the fruit would collapse when stirred into the cake batter. Allow the blackcurrants to cool. Meanwhile, line the cups of a six-cup microwave muffin tray or six small ramekins with two paper bun cases each, one inside the other.

In a bowl, sift the flour with the baking powder, adding the grains left in the sieve. Blend in the milk, brown sugar, oil and egg. Carefully fold in the blackcurrants, taking care not to crush them.

Using one third of the blackcurrant mixture, half-fill the six paper cases. Microwave on high for 2½ to 3 minutes, giving the tray a half turn after 1½ minutes, or rearranging the ramekins once.

Meanwhile, mix the brown sugar with the cinnamon for the topping. As soon as the muffins have been removed from the oven, sprinkle each one with a little of the topping. Discard the outer paper case from each muffin and let the muffins cool on a rack. Cook the remaining two batches of muffins in the same way.

EDITOR'S NOTE: *These American-style muffins freeze well and can be thawed quickly in the microwave. To reheat two frozen muffins, cook them on high for ½ to ¾ minutes, until just warm to the touch. Four muffins need 1 to 1½ minutes and six need 2 to 3 minutes. Leave the muffins to stand for 3 minutes before serving them.*

Upside-Down Apple Ring

THIS CAKE, WITH ITS PUDDING-LIKE TEXTURE, IS GOOD SERVED
WARM FOR BREAKFAST.

Serves: 12
Working time: about 20 minutes
Total time: about 35 minutes

Calories **215**
Protein **4g**
Cholesterol **1mg**
Total fat **10g**
Saturated fat **2g**
Sodium **175mg**

4	digestive biscuits, crushed	4
2	dessert apples, peeled, cored and sliced	2
125 g	polyunsaturated margarine	4 oz
90 g	dark brown sugar	3 oz
2	egg whites, lightly beaten	2
15 cl	plain low-fat yogurt	¼ pint
250 g	wholemeal flour	8 oz
1 tsp	baking powder	1 tsp
1 tbsp	ground mixed spice	1 tbsp
1	cooking apple, peeled, cored and grated	1

Grease a 22 cm (9 inch) flat-based tube mould and sprinkle it with the biscuit crumbs to coat its inner surface. Arrange the apple slices in the base of the mould, overlapping them slightly.

In a large bowl, cream the margarine with the sugar, egg whites and yogurt. Sift in the flour with the baking powder and mixed spice, adding the bran left in the sieve. Fold the dry ingredients and the grated apple into the creamed mixture. Spoon the batter into the prepared ring mould and spread it evenly.

Microwave on medium high for 8 to 10 minutes, giving the dish a quarter turn every 2 minutes. The cake is cooked when it feels springy to the touch. Leave it to stand for 5 minutes before turning it out. Serve the apple ring warm or cold.

SUGGESTED ACCOMPANIMENT: *sweetened Greek yogurt.*

Gingerbread Squares with Crystallized Pineapple

IF THIS GINGERBREAD IS KEPT IN A TIN FOR A DAY OR TWO, THE HONEY IN IT ABSORBS VAPOUR FROM THE AIR AND THE CAKE BECOMES DELICIOUSLY MOIST.

Serves 15
Working time: about 15 minutes
Total time: about 2 hours

Calories **230**
Protein **4g**
Cholesterol **35mg**
Total fat **8g**
Saturated fat **2g**
Sodium **115mg**

250 g	wholemeal flour	8 oz
1 tbsp	ground ginger	1 tbsp
1 tsp	ground mixed spice	1 tsp
½ tsp	bicarbonate of soda	½ tsp
125 g	polyunsaturated margarine	4 oz
125 g	clear honey	4 oz
1 tbsp	molasses	1 tbsp
125 g	muscovado sugar	4 oz
15 cl	skimmed milk	¼ pint
	eggs	2
1 tbsp	crystallized pineapple, chopped	1 tbsp

Lightly grease a 22 by 18 cm (9 by 7 inch) dish. Line the base with greaseproof paper.

Sift the flour into a bowl, together with the ginger, mixed spice and bicarbonate of soda. Add the bran left in the sieve. Put the margarine and all but 1 teaspoon of the honey in another bowl. Add the molasses and muscovado sugar, and microwave on high for 3 minutes, stirring once. Allow the mixture to cool slightly, then blend in the milk and eggs.

Make a well in the centre of the dry ingredients and pour in the liquid mixture. Beat well to create a smooth, thick batter. Spoon the batter evenly into the dish and set the dish on an inverted plate in the microwave. Cook on high for 7½ to 8½ minutes, giving the dish a quarter turn every 2 minutes. The gingerbread is done when it is springy to the touch and any damp spots have disappeared from its surface. Leave it to stand for 10 minutes before turning it out of the dish to cool on a wire rack.

Put the remaining honey in a small bowl and microwave it on high for 10 to 15 seconds. To glaze the gingerbread, brush it with the warm honey. Cut the gingerbread into squares and decorate each one with a few pieces of crystallized pineapple.

Date and Banana Tea Bread

Serves 12
Working time: about 20 minutes
Total time: about 1 hour

Calories **145**
Protein **3g**
Cholesterol **25mg**
Total fat **6g**
Saturated fat **3g**
Sodium **115mg**

125 g	wholemeal flour	4 oz
1 tsp	bicarbonate of soda	1 tsp
2	bananas, mashed	2
4 tbsp	plain low-fat yogurt	4 tbsp
60 g	light brown sugar	2 oz
75 g	unsalted butter	2½ oz
1	egg, beaten	1
2 tbsp	maple syrup	2 tbsp
90 g	dried dates, stoned, coarsely chopped	3 oz
	icing sugar	

Lightly grease a 22 by 12 cm (9 by 5 inch) loaf dish and line the base with greaseproof paper. Sift the whole-meal flour with the bicarbonate of soda, adding the bran left in the sieve.

Mix the bananas with the yogurt, brown sugar, butter, egg and syrup, blending well with a wooden spoon. Add the flour mixture and dates and mix to a smooth batter. Spoon the mixture evenly into the loaf dish. To prevent the ends of the cake from overcooking, wrap a 5 cm (2 inch) wide strip of foil over each end of the dish. Place the dish on an inverted plate in the microwave and cook on medium for 10 minutes, giving the dish a quarter turn every 2½ minutes.

Increase the power to high and microwave for a further 2 minutes. Remove the foil, give the dish a quarter turn and cook for a further 1 to 3 minutes until the tea bread shrinks from the sides of the dish. Leave the tea bread to stand for 10 minutes before turning it out on a wire rack. Sift a light coating of icing sugar over the cake and serve it warm or cold.

Spiced Apple Tea Bread

MUSCOVADO SUGAR GIVES THIS TEA BREAD THE RICH, DARK
COLOUR OF AN OVEN-BAKED CAKE: UNLIKE TRADITIONAL CAKES,
MICROWAVED CAKES NEVER BROWN ON THE SURFACE.

Serves 12
Working time: about 30 minutes
Total time: about 2 hours

Calories **185**
Protein **3g**
Cholesterol **45mg**
Total fat **6g**
Saturated fat **1g**
Sodium **105mg**

250 g	dessert apples, peeled, cored and chopped	8 oz
4 tsp	fresh lemon juice	4 tsp
75 g	plain flour	2½ oz
75 g	wholemeal flour	2½ oz
1¼ tsp	bicarbonate of soda	1¼ tsp
2 tsp	ground cinnamon	2 tsp
½ tsp	grated nutmeg	½ tsp
125 g	muscovado sugar	4 oz
125 g	raisins	4 oz
4 tbsp	safflower oil	4 tbsp
2	eggs, beaten	2
Apple topping		
1	large red dessert apple, cored, halved and thinly sliced	1
2 tsp	lemon juice	2 tsp
1 tbsp	apricot jam without added sugar	1 tbsp

Lightly grease a 22 by 12 cm (9 by 5 inch) glass loaf dish and line the base with greaseproof paper.

Place the chopped apples and 2 teaspoons of the lemon juice in a bowl. Cover the fruit and microwave it on high for 4 minutes, stirring once. Purée it in a blender or pass it through a fine sieve.

Meanwhile, sift the flours with the bicarbonate of soda, cinnamon and nutmeg into a bowl, adding the bran left in the sieve. Stir in the muscovado sugar, raisins, oil, beaten eggs, puréed apple and remaining lemon juice, and beat the mixture to a smooth batter with a wooden spoon. Spoon the mixture evenly into the prepared loaf dish. To prevent the ends of the cake from overcooking, wrap a 5 cm (2 inch) wide strip of foil over each end of the dish. Stand the dish on an inverted plate in the microwave oven and cook the cake on medium for 9 minutes, giving the dish a quarter turn every 3 minutes.

Increase the power to high and microwave for a further 2 minutes. Remove the foil, give the dish a quarter turn and microwave on high for a further 1 to 3 minutes. The tea bread will be cooked when it shrinks from the sides of the dish and no raw mixture can be seen through the bottom of the dish. Leave the tea bread to stand for 10 minutes before turning it out on to a wire rack to cool.

To make the apple topping, toss the apple slices in one teaspoon of the lemon juice in a shallow dish. Microwave the slices on high for 1 minute, then let them cool. Meanwhile, blend the jam with the remaining lemon juice in a bowl and microwave the mixture on high for 15 to 30 seconds to warm it. Sieve it, then brush half the jam mixture over the cake. Arrange the apple slices on the cake and glaze them with the remaining jam mixture.

Carrot and Walnut Cake

THE FRUCTOSE IN THIS RECIPE POSSESSES ONE AND A HALF TIMES
THE SWEETENING POWER AS THE SAME WEIGHT OF SUGAR, BUT
CONTRIBUTES THE SAME NUMBER OF CALORIES.

Serves 8
Working time: about 30 minutes
Total time: about 2 hours

Calories **230**
Protein **2g**
Cholesterol **65mg**
Total fat **12g**
Saturated fat **2g**
Sodium **225mg**

175 g	carrots, finely grated	6 oz
8 cl	safflower oil	3 fl oz
2 tbsp	skimmed milk	2 tbsp
2	eggs, beaten	2
90 g	fructose	3 oz
90 g	plain flour	3 oz
1 tsp	baking powder	1 tsp
1 tsp	bicarbonate of soda	1 tsp
2 tsp	ground cinnamon	2 tsp
90 g	raisins	3 oz
15 g	shelled walnuts, chopped	½ oz
	icing sugar (optional)	

Grease an 18 cm (7 inch) round cake dish and line it with greaseproof paper.

In a large bowl, mix the carrots well with the oil, skimmed milk, eggs and fructose. Sift in the flour together with the baking powder, bicarbonate of soda and cinnamon. Fold the dry mixture into the egg mixture, and blend in the raisins and walnuts. Spoon the batter into the cake dish.

Place the cake dish on an inverted saucer in the microwave. Cook the carrot cake on medium for 9 minutes, giving the dish a quarter turn every 3 minutes. Increase the power to high and microwave the cake for 2 to 3 minutes more, giving the dish a quarter turn after 1½ minutes. The cake is cooked when it shrinks from the sides of the dish. Leave the cake to stand for 10 minutes before turning it out of the dish to cool on a wire rack.

If you wish to decorate the cake, rest a wire rack on top of it and sift a little icing sugar over the cake from a sieve. Lift off the rack to reveal a stencil pattern.

Grapefruit Cake

Serves 12
Working time: about 30 minutes
Total time: about 3 hours

Calories **240**
Protein **4g**
Cholesterol **65mg**
Total fat **8g**
Saturated fat **2g**
Sodium **100mg**

125 g	sultanas	4 oz
125 g	raisins	4 oz
125 g	currants	4 oz
1	grapefruit, rind finely grated, flesh segmented (page 14) and chopped	1
10 cl	fresh grapefruit juice	3½ fl oz
90 g	polyunsaturated margarine	3 oz
90 g	dark brown sugar	3 oz
2	large eggs, beaten	2
175 g	plain flour	6 oz
1 tbsp	clear honey	1 tbsp

Grease the base of an 18 cm (7 inch) round cake dish and line it with greaseproof paper.

Put the sultanas, raisins, currants, grapefruit rind and juice in a bowl. Cover the fruit and microwave it on high for 3 minutes, stirring once. Remove the cover and leave the fruit to cool slightly.

Meanwhile, in another bowl, cream the margarine with the sugar and eggs until light and fluffy. Fold in the flour and the dried fruit mixture, blending well. Lastly, fold in the grapefruit flesh. Spoon the mixture into the cake dish and level the surface.

Cover the dish and place it on an inverted plate in the microwave. Cook the cake on high for 10 minutes, giving the dish a quarter turn every 3 minutes. Remove the cover, reduce the power to defrost and cook for a further 4 to 6 minutes — or until a skewer inserted into the centre of the cake comes out clean.

Leave the grapefruit cake to stand for 20 minutes before turning it out on to a wire rack to cool. While the cake is still warm, brush the top with the honey.

EDITOR'S NOTE: *One grapefruit will yield about 10 cl (3½ fl oz) of juice.*

Banana Loaf with Streusel Crumbs

Serves 12
Working time: about 20 minutes
Total time: about 2 hours

Calories **245**
Protein **5g**
Cholesterol **45mg**
Total fat **11g**
Saturated fat **2g**
Sodium **145mg**

100 g	wholemeal flour	3½ oz
60 g	plain flour	2 oz
1 tsp	bicarbonate of soda	1 tsp
90 g	fructose	3 oz
60 g	sultanas	2 oz
60 g	shelled hazelnuts, chopped	2 oz
4 tbsp	safflower oil	4 tbsp
1	small dessert apple, peeled, cored and grated	1
6 tbsp	skimmed milk	6 tbsp
2	eggs, beaten	2
2	ripe bananas, mashed	2
Streusel topping		
60 g	wholemeal flour	2 oz
60 g	muscovado sugar	2 oz
½ tsp	ground mixed spice	½ tsp
30 g	polyunsaturated margarine	1 oz

Lightly grease a 22 by 12 cm (9 by 5 inch) glass loaf dish and line the base with greaseproof paper.

In a bowl, sift the flours with the bicarbonate of soda, adding the bran left in the sieve. Stir in the fructose, sultanas and hazelnuts. Mix the oil with the apple, milk, eggs and bananas, then add the mixture to the dry ingredients and beat with a wooden spoon.

To make the streusel topping, mix the flour with the sugar and mixed spice. Rub in the margarine until the mixture resembles fine breadcrumbs.

Spoon the banana mixture evenly into the loaf dish and sprinkle it with the streusel topping. To prevent the ends of the loaf from overcooking, wrap a 5 cm (2 inch) wide strip of foil over each end of the dish. Place the dish on an inverted plate in the microwave and cook the loaf on medium for 9 minutes, giving the dish a quarter turn every 3 minutes.

Increase the power to high and microwave the loaf for a further 2 minutes. Remove the foil, give the dish a quarter turn and cook for a further 2 to 4 minutes until the loaf shrinks from the sides of the dish and no uncooked mixture can be seen through the bottom of the dish. Leave the cake to stand for 10 minutes before turning it out on to a wire rack to cool.

Cheesecake with Strawberries and Kiwi Fruit

Serves 10
Working time: about 40 minutes
Total time: about 3 hours

Calories **175**
Protein **9g**
Cholesterol **65mg**
Total fat **7g**
Saturated fat **1g**
Sodium **120mg**

90 g	digestive biscuits, crushed	3 oz
125 g	low-fat ricotta cheese	4 oz
250 g	quark	8 oz
2	eggs, whites and yolks separated	2
1 tbsp	wholemeal flour	1 tbsp
3 tbsp	clear honey	3 tbsp
2 tsp	fresh orange juice	2 tsp
15 cl	plain low-fat yogurt	¼ pint
60 g	sultanas, chopped	2 oz
4	large strawberries, hulled and sliced	4
2	kiwi fruits, peeled and sliced	2

Grease an 18 cm (7 inch) flan dish. Line the base with greaseproof paper and grease the paper. Spread the biscuit crumbs on the base and flatten the biscuit layer with the back of a spoon.

Put the ricotta in a bowl with the quark, egg yolks, flour, honey, orange juice and yogurt and beat with a wooden spoon until the mixture is smooth. Microwave the mixture on medium for 7 to 8 minutes or until thick, whisking it every 2 minutes.

Stir the sultanas into the mixture. Whisk the egg whites until they stand in stiff peaks and fold them into the cheesecake mixture. Spoon the mixture evenly over the biscuit base.

Microwave the cheesecake on medium for 10 to 12 minutes, or until it is just set in the centre, giving the dish a quarter turn every 3 minutes. Leave the cheesecake to stand until cool, then put the dish in the refrigerator for about 2 hours to chill the cake and make it firm enough to unmould.

Run a knife round the cheesecake to loosen it from the sides of the dish. Put a flat plate over the cheesecake and invert plate and dish together. Lift off the dish, remove the paper from the base of the cheesecake and turn it on to a serving dish. Decorate the top with the slices of strawberry and kiwi fruit.

Orange and Lemon Ring Cake

THE FRUCTOSE IN THIS RECIPE POSSESSES ONE AND A HALF TIMES
THE SWEETENING POWER AS THE SAME WEIGHT OF SUGAR, BUT
CONTRIBUTES THE SAME NUMBER OF CALORIES.

Serves: 10
Working time: about 30 minutes
Total time: about 1 hour and 30 minutes

Calories **225**
Protein **5g**
Cholesterol **80mg**
Total fat **11g**
Saturated fat **2g**
Sodium **170mg**

4	digestive biscuits, crushed	4
75 g	fructose	2½ oz
3	eggs, beaten	3
8 cl	safflower oil	3 fl oz
½	lemon, grated rind only	½
½	small orange, grated rind only	½
2 tbsp	fresh lemon juice	2 tbsp
2 tbsp	fresh orange juice	2 tbsp
175 g	plain flour	6 oz
2 tsp	baking powder	2 tsp
Orange garnish and glaze		
1	large orange, peel and all pith removed (page 14)	1
1 tbsp	honey	1 tbsp

Lightly grease a 2 litre (3½ pint) fluted ring mould and coat it evenly with the biscuit crumbs. Put the fructose, eggs, oil, grated rind and juice into a bowl, sift in the flour and baking powder, and whisk them with an electric beater at low speed for about 30 seconds, until well blended and smooth.

Spoon the mixture into the prepared ring mould, taking care not to disturb the biscuit crumb coating. Microwave the cake on high for 4 to 5 minutes, giving the mould a quarter turn every minute, until the cake feels springy to the touch.

Leave the cake to stand for 10 minutes before turning it out on to a wire rack. While the cake cools, prepare the garnish. Slice the orange into segments, cutting on either side of the membrane *(page 14)*; hold the orange over a bowl to catch the juice. To soften the segments, put them in a dish and microwave them on high for 1 to 1½ minutes. Add any juice that escapes from them to the juice already in the bowl.

To make the glaze, combine the honey with the juice from the orange and microwave the mixture on high for 30 seconds. When the cake is cool, brush it with the honey-orange glaze and decorate it with the orange segments.

Chocolate and Apricot Roulade

ROULADES COOKED IN THE MICROWAVE OVEN DO NOT NEED TO BE TRIMMED BEFORE ROLLING BECAUSE THE MICROWAVE, UNLIKE A CONVENTIONAL OVEN, DOES NOT MAKE THE EDGES OF THE SPONGE CRISP AND BRITTLE DURING COOKING.

Serves 8
Working time: about 50 minutes
Total time: about 2 hours and 15 minutes

Calories **170**
Protein **4g**
Cholesterol **70mg**
Total fat **10g**
Saturated fat **5g**
Sodium **100mg**

2	large eggs	2
75 g	caster sugar	2½ oz
45 g	plain flour	1½ oz
4 tsp	cocoa powder	4 tsp
10 cl	double cream	3½ fl oz
200 g	fromage frais	7 oz
90 g	fresh apricots, halved, stoned, poached and skinned (page 14)	3 oz

Line a 28 by 18 cm (11 by 7 inch) shallow rectangular dish with lightly oiled greaseproof paper, leaving about 5 cm (2 inches) of paper overlapping at the edges.

Whisk the eggs with 50 g (1¾ oz) of the sugar until very thick and trebled in volume. Sift the flour with the cocoa powder twice, then sift the combination over the whisked egg. Fold the two mixtures together lightly with a metal spoon and pour the batter into the prepared dish, spreading it evenly.

Microwave the sponge on high for 2½ to 3 minutes until it is just firm in the centre, giving the dish a half turn once. Leave the cake to stand for 3 minutes.

Dust a sheet of greaseproof paper with 15 g (½ oz) of the caster sugar, which will help prevent the moist sponge from sticking. Turn the cake out on to the sugared paper. Remove the lining paper. Hold another piece of greaseproof paper under a tap to dampen it; crumple it up, spread it out again and lay it on the sponge. Roll the sponge up from one of the shorter edges, enclosing the paper (page 31). Allow the cake to cool on a wire rack.

Meanwhile, whip the cream until it stands in peaks, then blend in the fromage frais. Transfer one tablespoon of the cream and cheese mixture to a piping bag fitted with a medium-sized star nozzle. Set aside a few slivers from one apricot half for decoration. Chop the remaining apricots and stir them into the rest of the cream and cheese mixture.

Unroll the roulade and remove the paper. Spread the sponge with the apricot and cream mixture, roll up the sponge again to enclose the filling and place the cake, seam side down, on a serving plate. Sprinkle the roulade with the remaining 10 g (¼ oz) sugar to cover any surface blemishes. Pipe the remaining cream mixture along the top of the roulade in swirls and decorate the cake with the reserved apricot slivers. Chill the roulade in the refrigerator for about 1 hour to make it firm enough to slice. Just before serving, trim the ends of the roll.

Raspberry and Hazelnut Roulade

Serves 8
Working time: about 45 minutes
Total time: about 2 hours and 15 minutes

Calories **180**
Protein **5g**
Cholesterol **70mg**
Total fat **12g**
Saturated fat **6g**
Sodium **70mg**

2	large eggs	2
60 g	caster sugar	2 oz
60 g	plain flour, sifted twice	2 oz
45 g	shelled hazelnuts, ground	1½ oz
12.5 cl	double cream	4 fl oz
1	egg white	1
175 g	fresh raspberries, or frozen raspberries, thawed	6 oz

Line a 28 by 18 cm (11 by 7 inch) shallow rectangular dish with lightly oiled greaseproof paper, leaving about 5 cm (2 inches) of paper overlapping at the edges.

Whisk the eggs and caster sugar in a bowl until the mixture is very thick and has trebled in volume. Sift the flour over the egg mixture and fold it in with a metal spoon. Pour the batter into the paper-lined dish, spreading it evenly.

Microwave the cake on high for 2½ to 3 minutes, until it is just firm in the centre, giving the dish a half turn once. Leave the cake to stand for 3 minutes.

Sprinkle a sheet of greaseproof paper with the hazelnuts. Turn the sponge out on to the hazelnuts. Remove the lining paper. Hold another piece of greaseproof paper under a tap for a few seconds to dampen it; crumple it up, spread it out again and lay it on top of the sponge. Roll the cake up from one of the shorter edges, enclosing the paper *(page 31)*. Let the cake cool on a wire rack.

Meanwhile, whip the cream until it stands in soft peaks. In another bowl, beat the egg white until stiff and fold it into the cream.

Unroll the sponge, remove the paper, spread the cream over the surface and dot it with the raspberries. Roll up the cake again and place it on a serving plate, seam side down. Chill the roulade in the refrigerator for at least 1 hour, until it becomes firm enough to slice. Just before serving, trim the ends.

Glossary

Allspice: the dried berry of a member of the myrtle family. Used whole or ground, it is called allspice because its flavour resembles a combination of clove, cinnamon and nutmeg.

Amaretto: an almond-flavoured liqueur.

Angel food cake: very light cake with a snow white crumb, it is aerated with beaten egg whites and contains no fat or egg yolks.

Angelica: the stalk of the angelica plant that has been candied in sugar syrup. Cut into delicate shapes, it is used to decorate cakes.

Armagnac: a dry brandy, often more strongly flavoured than cognac, from the Armagnac district of south-west France.

Arrowroot: a tasteless, starchy, white powder refined from the root of a tropical plant; it is used to thicken purées and sauces. Unlike flour, it is transparent when cooked.

Baking powder: a raising agent that releases carbon dioxide during baking, causing cake or biscuit batter to rise. Ordinary baking powders, as used in these recipes, have a high sodium content, but low-sodium baking powder is available for people on restricted-sodium diets.

Bicarbonate of soda: a raising agent in cake-making, it is activated when combined with an acidic ingredient such as vinegar or black treacle.

Black treacle: molasses cleaned of impurities such as waxes and cane fibre. See also Molasses.

Brown flour: wheat flour which contains about 85% of the wheat grain; some of the bran and germ has been removed.

Brown sugars: ranging in colour from pale beige to dark brown, brown sugars are often prepared by purifying raw cane sugar to some degree. Alternatively brown sugar is made from fully refined white sugar mingled with molasses. Nutritionally, brown sugars have only a fractional advantage over white sugars but they are valued for their stronger flavour.

Buckwheat flour: a strongly flavoured flour made from roasted buckwheat seeds.

Buttermilk: a tangy, cultured milk product that, despite its name, contains about one third less fat than whole milk.

Calorie (or kilocalorie): a precise measure of the energy food supplies when it is broken down for use in the body.

Caramelize: to heat sugar, or a food naturally rich in sugar such as fruit, until the sugar turns brown and syrupy.

Cardamom: the bittersweet, aromatic dried seeds or whole pods of a plant in the ginger family. Cardamom seeds may be used whole or ground.

Cholesterol: a waxlike substance that is manufactured in the human body and also found in foods of animal origin. Although a certain amount of cholesterol is necessary for proper body functioning, an excess can accumulate in the arteries, contributing to heart disease. See also Monounsaturated fats; Polyunsaturated fats; Saturated fats.

Cocoa powder: the result of pulverizing roasted cocoa beans, then removing most of the fat, or cocoa butter.

Cornflour: a starchy white powder made from corn kernels and used to thicken many puddings and sauces. Like arrowroot, it is transparent when cooked and makes a more efficient thickener than flour. When cooked conventionally, a liquid containing cornflour must be stirred constantly in the early stages to prevent lumps from forming.

Cottage cheese: a low-fat soft cheese with a mild flavour and a non-uniform texture. It is made from skimmed milk, but the cottage cheese used in this book has added cream to give it a fat content of 4 per cent.

Cream of tartar: a natural, mild acid in powder form with a slightly sour taste, used to strengthen beaten egg whites. It should be used sparingly — no more than 1/8 teaspoon to one egg white. Beating whites in a copper bowl has a similar strengthening effect.

Creamed coconut: coconut flesh which has been dried and pressed into blocks.

Curd cheese: any soft cheese made from separated milk curds; it may be used in cheesecakes and as a low-fat cake topping. The medium-fat curd cheese used in this book contains 12 per cent fat.

Dates: the fruit of the date palm, dates can be bought fresh or dried. When dried dates are specified, choose plump unstoned dates in preference to pressed slab dates.

Demerara sugar: a large-crystal brown sugar. See also Brown sugars.

Dietary fibre: a plant-cell material that passes undigested through the human body, but promotes healthy digestion of other food matter. The fibre in this book is provided mainly by the bran in wholemeal flour and by fresh and dried fruits.

Fat: a basic component of many foods, comprising three types of fatty acid — saturated, monounsaturated and polyunsaturated — in varying proportions. See also Monounsaturated fats; Polyunsaturated fats; Saturated fats.

Fibre: see Dietary fibre.

Filbert: see Hazelnut.

Fromage frais: a soft smooth cheese made from skimmed milk. The *fromage frais* used in this book includes a small proportion of added cream and has an 8 per cent fat content.

Fructose: a sugar found in honey and many fruits, fructose is the sweetest of all natural sugars. It can be bought as a powder and looks much like ordinary caster sugar.

Gelatine: a virtually tasteless protein, available in powdered form or in sheets. Dissolved gelatine is used to set chilled cakes so that they retain their shape when unmoulded.

Ginger: the spicy, rootlike stem of the ginger plant, used as a cake flavouring either dried and powdered or preserved whole in syrup.

Glaze: to coat the surface of a tart or cake with a thin, shiny layer of melted jam or caramel.

Grand Marnier: a high-quality liqueur made from cognac and orange peel, which has a distinctive orange flavour.

Hazelnut: the fruit of a shrublike tree found primarily in Turkey, Italy and Spain, and in the United States. Filberts, which are cultivated, have a stronger flavour than hazelnuts, which grow wild. Both are prized by bakers and sweetmakers.

Icing sugar: finely ground granulated sugar, with a small amount of added cornflour to ensure a powdery consistency. Icing sugar's ability to dissolve instantly makes it ideal for cake icings, where a grainy texture is undesirable.

Jam without added sugar: jam which is sweetened by the sugar naturally found in fruit (fructose), rather than by added sugar (sucrose). Once opened it must be stored in the refrigerator, where it will keep for about three weeks.

Kirsch (also called Kirschwasser): a clear cherry brandy distilled from small black cherries grown in Switzerland, Germany and the Alsace region of France.

Kiwi fruit: an egg-shaped fruit with a fuzzy brown skin, tart, lime-green flesh and hundreds of tiny black edible seeds. Peeled and sliced horizontally, the kiwi displays a starburst of seeds at its centre that lends a decorative note to cake toppings.

Kugelhopf mould: a decoratively fluted tube cake tin. The tube conducts heat into the centre of the batter, ensuring even cooking.

Madeleine tray: a specialized mould with scallop-shaped indentations, designed for making small cakes.

Malt extract: a by-product of beer-making, containing the sugar maltose, which is much less sweet than sucrose. Malt extract has a strong flavour and retains moisture well.

Malted wheat flour: a brown flour with added grains of malted wheat which give it a crunchy texture and nutty flavour.

Mango: a fruit grown throughout the tropics, with sweet, succulent, yellow-orange flesh that is extremely rich in vitamin A. Like papaya, it may cause an allergic reaction in some individuals.

Maple syrup: a sweet, golden syrup produced from the sap of the maple tree.

Meringue: an airy concoction made from stiffly beaten egg whites and sugar. It can be baked to produce edible baskets, or be layered between sponge to make up a gateau.

Mixed candied peel: the peel of citrus fruit, soaked in a concentrated sugar solution. It can be bought whole, or already chopped.

Molasses: a thick, dark, strongly flavoured syrup, rich in iron and a good source of vitamin B. It is a by-product of sugar-cane refining.

Monounsaturated fats: one of the three types of fats found in foods. Monounsaturated fats are believed not to raise the level of cholesterol in the blood.

Muscovado sugar: originally, the name signified a brown sugar from the West Indian island of Barbados. Today the geographical connotation has gone, and the name is used for a mixture of unrefined sugar-cane juice and black treacle which is spun to produce a moist, dark brown sugar.

Papaya (also called pawpaw): a pear-shaped melon-like tropical fruit rich in vitamins A and C. Like mango, it may cause an allergic reaction in some individuals.

Parchment paper: a reusable paper treated with silicone to produce a non-stick surface. It is used to line cake tins and baking sheets.

Passion fruit: a juicy, fragrant, egg-shaped tropical fruit with wrinkled skin, yellow flesh and many small black seeds. The seeds are edible; the skin is not.

Pine-nuts: seeds from the cones of the stone pine, a tree native to the Mediterranean. Toasting brings out their buttery flavour.

Pistachio nuts: prized for their pleasant flavour and green colour, pistachio nuts must be shelled and boiled for a few minutes before their skins can be removed.

Poach: to cook a food in barely simmering liquid. Fruit may be poached in water or a light syrup.

Polyunsaturated fats: one of the three types of fats found in foods. They exist in abundance in such vegetable oils as safflower, sunflower, corn and soya. Polyunsaturated fats lower the level of cholesterol in the blood.

Poppy seeds: the spherical black seeds produced by a variety of poppy plant, and used as an ingredient or topping in cakes. Poppy seeds are so small that 500 g (1 lb) numbers nearly a million seeds.

Purée: to reduce food to a smooth, even, pulplike consistency by mashing it, passing it through a sieve, or processing it in a food processor or a blender.

Quark: a type of soft cheese with a mild, clean, slightly acid flavour; usually very low in fat, but smoother varieties have added cream.

Recommended Daily Amount (RDA): the average daily amount of an essential nutrient recommended for healthy people by the U.K. Department of Health and Social Security.

Reduce: to boil down a liquid in order to concentrate its flavour and thicken its consistency.

Ricotta: a soft, mild, white Italian cheese, made from cow's or sheep's milk. The low-fat ricotta used in this book has a fat content of about 8 per cent.

Rind: the flavourful outermost layer of citrus-fruit peel; it should be cut or grated free of the white pith that lies beneath it.

Ring mould or savarin mould: a circular cake tin with a hollow centre. Its open centre nearly doubles the food surfaces that are exposed to its metal walls,

thus speeding up the cooking time.

Rolled oats: a cereal made from oats that have been ground into meal, then steamed, rolled into flakes and dried.

Rose water: a flavouring produced by distilling the oil of rose petals.

Roulade: a light sponge mixture baked in a shallow rectangular tin, then turned out, spread with filling and rolled up.

Safflower oil: a vegetable oil that contains the highest proportion of polyunsaturated fats.

Saffron: the dried reddish stigmas of the crocus flower, saffron yields a pungent flavour and a bright yellow colour.

Saturated fats: one of the three types of fats found in foods. They exist in abundance in animal products and coconut and palm oils; they raise the level of cholesterol in the blood. Because high blood-cholesterol levels may cause heart disease, saturated fat consumption should be restricted to less than 15 per cent of the calories provided by the daily diet.

Savarin: a yeast-risen cake, soaked in sugar syrup and flavoured with rum or brandy. The cake is named after Brillat-Savarin, an 18th-century writer on gastronomical subjects.

Simmer: to maintain a liquid at a temperature just below its boiling point so that the liquid's surface barely ripples.

Skimmed milk: milk from which almost all the fat has been removed.

Sodium: a nutrient essential to maintaining the proper balance of fluids in the body. In most diets, a major source of the element is table salt, which contains 40 per cent sodium. Excess sodium may contribute to high blood pressure, which increases the risk of heart disease. One teaspoon (5.5 g) of salt, with 2,132 milligrams of sodium, contains just over the maximum daily amount recommended by the World Health Organization.

Springform tin: a round tin with removable sides,

designed to hold cakes and desserts that cannot be unmoulded.

Streusel: a topping for cakes, usually made by combining flour, butter, sugar and flavourings to form coarse crumbs.

Strong flour: a white flour milled from strains of wheat with a high protein content. The high proportion of protein, which combines with water to form gluten, makes for a cake of large volume and open texture. Strong flour is used mainly for yeast-risen mixtures.

Swiss roll tin: a shallow rectangular baking tin, about 2.5 cm (1 inch) deep, in which a roulade mixture is cooked.

Tofu: a low-fat high-protein curd made from soya beans. It looks like white cheese.

Total fat: an individual's daily intake of polyunsaturated, monounsaturated and saturated fats. Nutritionists recommend that total fat constitute no more than 35 per cent of the energy in the diet. The term as used in this book refers to the combined fats in a given dish or food.

Vanilla extract: pure vanilla extract is the flavouring obtained by macerating vanilla pods in an alcohol solution. Artificial vanilla flavouring is chemically synthesized from clove oil.

Vanilla sugar: sugar flavoured by placing a whole vanilla pod in a closed container of sugar for about a week.

Wholemeal flour: wheat flour which contains the whole of the wheat grain with nothing added or taken away. It is nutritionally valuable as a source of dietary fibre and it is higher in B vitamins than white flour.

Yeast: a micro-organism which feeds on sugars and starches to produce carbon dioxide and thus leaven a cake. Yeast can be bought either fresh or dried; fresh yeast will keep for up to six weeks in a refrigerator.

Yogurt: A smooth-textured, semi-solid cultured milk product. Low-fat yogurt contains about 1 per cent fat. Greek yogurt, which is made from full-cream milk, has a 10 per cent fat content.

Index

Picture Credits

Cover: Chris Knaggs. 4: top, Alan Duns; bottom left, Chris Knaggs; bottom right, Alan Duns. 5: top left, James Murphy; top right, John Elliott; bottom, James Murphy. 6: James Murphy. 10-11: John Elliott. 12-14: Chris Knaggs. 15: John Elliott. 17: Chris Knaggs, except for bottom left by John Elliott. 18: top and lower left, Chris Knaggs; lower right, John Elliott. 19: Chris Knaggs. 20-21: James Murphy. 22-23: Grant Symon. 24-27: Alan Duns. 28: James Murphy. 29: Alan Duns. 30: Grant Symon. 31: John Elliott. 32-33: Chris Knaggs. 35: John Elliott. 36: Tom Belshaw. 37: James Murphy. 38: Chris Knaggs. 39: John Elliott. 40: Alan Duns. 41-42: Tom Belshaw. 43: John Elliott. 44-46: Alan Duns. 47: Chris Knaggs. 48: John Elliott. 49-50: James Murphy. 51: Tom Belshaw. 52: Chris Knaggs. 53: Alan Duns. 54: John Elliott. 55: James Murphy. 56: Tom Belshaw. 57: James Murphy. 58-59: Tom Belshaw. 60: James Murphy. 61: Alan Duns. 62: John Elliott. 63: Tom Belshaw. 64-65: Chris Knaggs. 66-68: James Murphy. 69: Grant Symon. 70: John Elliott. 71: Chris Knaggs. 72: Alan Duns. 73-74: James Murphy. 75: Tom Belshaw. 76-77: Grant Symon. 78: Tom Belshaw. 79: Alan Duns. 80-81: Grant Symon. 82: Tom Belshaw. 83: Chris Knaggs. 84: John Elliott. 85: Tom Belshaw. 86: top: Alan Duns; bottom: John Elliott. 87: Chris Knaggs. 88: Rachel Andrew. 89: Chris Knaggs. 90-91: John Elliott. 92: Chris Knaggs. 93: John Elliott. 94-96: James Murphy. 97: John Elliott. 98: Chris Knaggs. 99: James Murphy. 100-101: Chris Knaggs. 102-103: John Elliott. 104: Chris Knaggs. 105: James Murphy. 106: Chris Knaggs. 107: James Murphy. 108: John Elliott. 109: James Murphy. 110-111: Chris Knaggs. 112-113: John Elliott. 114: James Murphy. 115: Chris Knaggs. 116: James Murphy. 117: John Elliott. 118-119: James Murphy. 120: John Elliott. 121-122: James Murphy. 123-139: John Elliott.

Props: The Editors wish to thank the following outlets and manufacturers; all are based in London unless otherwise stated. Cover: marble, W. E. Grant & Co. (Marble) Ltd.; 4: top: napkin, Kilkenny; bottom right: cup and saucer, David Mellor; napkin, Kilkenny; 5: top right: plate and fork, Villeroy & Boch; bottom: china, Fortnum & Mason; 24: pottery, Colin Kellan, The Craftsmen Potters Shop; knife, Next Interior; Napkin, Ewart Liddell; 25: plates, Hutschenreuther (U.K.) Ltd.; marble, W. E. Grant & Co. (Marble) Ltd.; 26: plates, Next Interior; place mat, Kilkenny; marble, W. E. Grant & Co. (Marble) Ltd.; 27: China, Royal Worcester, Worcester; napkin, Ewart Liddell; 28: Platter, Rosenthal (London) Ltd.; 29: cake stand, Thomas (London) Ltd.; 30: china, Villeroy & Boch; cake slice, Chinacraft Ltd.; marble, W. E. Grant & Co. (Marble) Ltd.; 32: platter, Villeroy & Boch; 40: napkin, Kilkenny; 41: plates, Anthony Phillips, The Craftsmen Potters Shop; cake slice, Mappin & Webb Silversmiths; 42: bowl, Birgit Blitz, Gruiten, Germany; marble, W. E. Grant & Co. (Marble) Ltd.; 43: bowl, Birgit Blitz, Gruiten, Germany; 46: China, Villeroy & Boch; tablecloth and napkin, Ewart Liddell; 47: plates, Villeroy & Boch; tablecloth, Laura Ashley Ltd.; 48: fabric, Osborne & Little plc; 51: fabric, Osborn & Little plc; 52: cup and saucer, Thomas (London) Ltd.; 53: cloth, Kilkenny; 54: knife, Next Interior; 55: marble, W. E. Grant & Co. (Marble) Ltd.; 56: cake slice and fork, Thomas (London) Ltd.; 57: plate, Royal Doulton, Stoke-on-Trent; fork, Mappin & Webb Silversmiths; tablecloth and napkin, Ewart Liddell; 59, china, Villeroy & Boch; forks, Mappin & Webb Silversmiths; 60: plate, Winchcombe Pottery, The Craftsmen Potters Shop; 61: knife, Next Interior; marble, W. E. Grant & Co. (Marble) Ltd.; 62: basket, Kilkenny; 63: plates, Next Interior; napkins and placemat, Kilkenny; 66-67: platter, Rosenthal (London) Ltd.; 68: plate, Villeroy & Boch; basket, Next Interior; 70: cake slice, Mappin & Webb Silversmiths; 71: plate, Chinacraft Ltd.; napkin, Kilkenny; 72: cup and saucer, David Mellor; napkin, Kilkenny; 74: marble, W. E. Grant & Co. (Marble) Ltd.; 75: cake plate, Rosenthal (London) Ltd.; napkin, Kilkenny; 78: china, Fortnum & Mason; forks, Mappin & Webb Silversmiths; tablecloth, Ewart Liddell; 79: platter, Rosenthal (London) Ltd.; cake slice, Mappin & Webb Silversmiths; tablecloth, Ewart Liddell; 80: platter, Thomas (London) Ltd.; marble, W. E. Grant & Co. (Marble) Ltd.; 81: plates, Fortnum & Mason; fork, Mappin & Webb Silversmiths; 82: plate, Thomas (London) Ltd.; napkin, Ewart Liddell; marble, W. E. Grant & Co. (Marble) Ltd.; 83: plates, Wedgwood; 84: plate, Hutschenreuther (U.K.) Ltd.; tablecloth, Ewart Liddell; 85: plate, Thomas (London) Ltd.; napkin, Kilkenny; marble, W. E. Grant & Co. (Marble) Ltd.; 86: fabric, Osborn & Little plc; 87: platter, Rosenthal (London) Ltd.; 89: china, Chinacraft Ltd.; tablecloth, Ewart Liddell; 90: plates, Hutschenreuther (U.K.) Ltd.; cake slice, Mappin & Webb Silversmiths; tablecloth (blue), Kilkenny; 92: china, Villeroy & Boch; tablecloth and napkin, Ewart Liddell; 93: tablecloth and napkin, Ewart Liddell; 96: marble, W. E. Grant & Co. (Marble) Ltd.; 97: napkin, Kilkenny; 98: top: platter, Thomas (London) Ltd.; marble, W. E. Grant & Co. (Marble) Ltd.; bottom: tablecloth, Next Interior; 99: marble, W. E. Grant & Co. (Marble) Ltd.; 100: pottery, Kilkenny; 102: plates, David Mellor; napkins, Kilkenny; tiles, Tilemart Ltd.; 103: china, Villeroy & Boch; 104: plates, Rosenthal (London) Ltd.; 105: china, Fortnum & Mason; knife, Mappin & Webb Silversmiths; tablecloth, Ewart Liddell; 108: plate, David Mellor; 110: platter, Thomas (London) Ltd.; 111: fabric, Liberty; 112: china, Line of Scandinavia; tablecloth and napkin, Kilkenny; 114: tablecloth and napkin, Kilkenny; 115: tablecloth, Next Interior; 116: platter, Rosenthal (London) Ltd.; 117: china, Royal Worcester, Worcester; place mat, Ewart Liddell; tablecloth, Laura Ashley; 118: plates, Thomas (London) Ltd.; 119: plates, Fortnum & Mason; forks, Mappin & Webb Silversmiths; napkin, Ewart Liddell; 121: plates, Royal Worcester, Worcester; tablecloth, Ewart Liddell; 122: plate, Hutschenreuther (U.K.) Ltd.; 125: china, Villeroy & Boch; lace cloth, Laura Ashley; tablecloth, Ewart Liddell; fork, Mappin & Webb Silversmiths; 126: china, Royal Worcester, Worcester; tablecloth and napkins, Laura Ashley; 128: teapot, platter and teaspoon, David Mellor; 129: basket, David Mellor; 130: plate, A. & J. Young, the Craftsmen Potters Shop; wooden platter, David Mellor; tablecloth and napkins, Kilkenny; 133: basket and platter, David Mellor; 136: cake slice, Thomas (London) Ltd.; marble, W. E. Grant & Co. (Marble) Ltd.; 137: small plate, fork and napkin ring, Villeroy & Boch; 138: pottery, Jack Doherty, The Craftsmen Potters Shop; 139: platter, plate and fork, Villeroy & Boch; tablecloth and napkins, Kilkenny.

Acknowledgements

The index for this book was prepared by Myra Clark. The editors also wish to thank: Judy Baylis, London; Rene Bloom, London; Andrew Cameron, London; Alexandra Carlier, London; John Costelloe, London; Stuart Cullen, London; Elizabeth David Ltd., London; Sean Davis, London; Formica, Newcastle, Tyne and Wear; Hilary Hockman, London; Elizabeth Hodgson, London; Rod Howe, London; Samuel Inwood, London; Johnson Brothers, Stoke-on-Trent; Giles Johnson, London; Lagostina and Le Creuset, The Kitchenware Merchants Ltd., London; Paul Moon, London; Christine Noble, London; Oneida, London; Penhallow Marketing Ltd, Sheffield, Yorkshire; Perstorp Warerite Ltd., London; Royal Copenhagen Porcelain and Georg Jensen Silversmiths (Ltd.), London; Sharp Electronics (U.K.) Ltd., London; Toshiba (U.K.) Ltd., London; Rita Walters, Seven Kings, Essex.

Colour Separations by Fotolitomec, S.N.C., Milan, Italy
Typesetting by G. Beard & Son Ltd., Brighton, Sussex, England
Printed in Italy by New Interlitho S.p.A. - Milan